MY PLUG

IN YOUR

SOCKET

AN AUTOBIOGRAPHICAL ACCOUNT
OF MY WORKING LIFE
(OR SOME OF IT AT LEAST)

BY

A. LECTRICIAN

(THAT IS A PSEUDONYM, NOT MY REAL NAME)

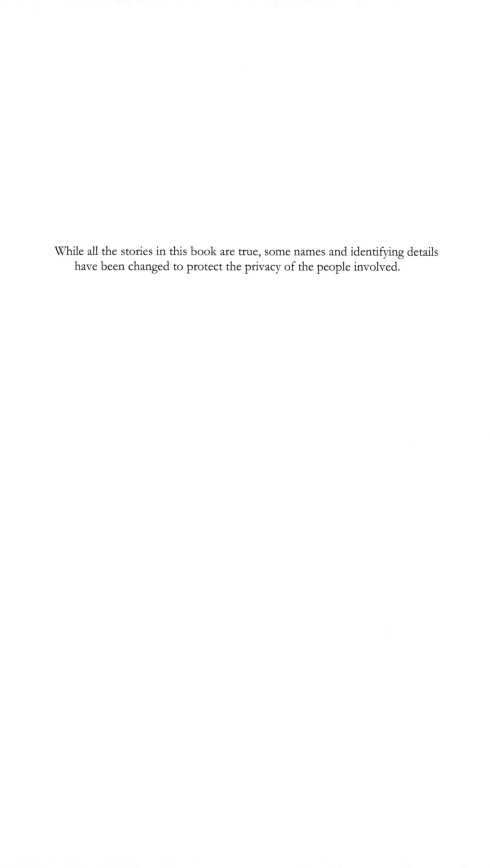

WRITTEN WITHOUT PREJUDICE
(WELL MOSTLY ANYWAY)

I would like to dedicate this book to the following people:

Me – for writing it. I could not have done it without myself.

My mum and dad, without whom I would not have existed.

My wife – for putting up with me and reading the draft copy, armed with a big red pen (a bit like being back at school really).

Mark Evill – he knows who he is, (if he is still alive) – believe me I tried every way I could to contact him – to whom I owe a lot of thanks for his arduous work, determination and dedication.

NB: I have since been, and am, in touch with Mark. I will not change the above dedication as it means a lot to me, as does he.

Jeanette Horton – for supplying the title of the book.

Geoffrey Alan Smith – Smiffy – for supplying the front cover (I let his imagination run riot). This may not be relevant if the publishing company create new artwork, but I will keep it anyway for his effort.

My grandchildren – Charlie, Mason, Connor, Rosie, Sonny and Maisie – for giving me the inspiration – and costing me a fortune.

All the people who I have encountered in my working life who gave me the stimulation – and the ammunition needed.

All my friends who will buy this book (hopefully) and recommend it to their friends.

Everyone else who buys a copy (all donations gratefully accepted – I need the money).

Everybody who knows me – (that is just practice in case it gets turned into a film and I get an Oscar or something).

CONTENTS

FOREWORD

ACTUALLY, THERE ARE MORE THAN FOUR WORDS BUT APPARENTLY THAT IS WHAT YOU HAVE AT THE BEGINNING OF A BOOK.

I am just an ordinary guy, from an ordinary background, leading an ordinary life – so why write a book? – an extraordinary book, 'some' would say! I know, I was that 'some'.

Two main reasons really:

After spending my working life on building sites all over Great Britain – and indeed sometimes further afield, even sometimes in the middle of a field – I just had to recall some of the 'characters' I have had the 'privilege'? to meet along the way and some of the (mostly funny) encounters that have arisen – either by accident or design.

The other reason is Charlie. My first and (at present) only grandchild. I thought it would be nice for him to have an insight into what went before. It has transpired that it has taken that long that I now have six wonderful grandchildren – see dedications.

Twice in my life I have had a near brush with death and know fully how mortal we are, so I decided to put it down in words before I end up shovelling coal into a furnace for eternity – let us face it, if all the good ones go to heaven it will be far more fun downstairs.

I have always read a lot myself and thought I could at least make an attempt to bring pleasure to others by bringing to life my 'encounters'. All complaints (or praise) to the website please – I need the hits to encourage advertisers.

I have attempted to recall the situations as accurately as possible in most instances. A certain amount of 'poetic license' may have been added occasionally. As the inimitable Mark Twain said, 'Never let the truth get in the way of a good story.' Other than this, all is as I can remember (difficult to remember much when you are this old, but I am trying – some people have said very trying indeed).

Some if not all the names have been changed to protect the innocent – or as in some (if not most) cases – the guilty.

Footnote: – The grandchildren are now coming thick and fast at this time (September 2017 – *ad infinitum*) so I must mention Mason Alexander in Perth, Australia, Connor Stanley (Stanley, in memory of my dad who died two weeks before Connor was born) – in Kegworth, Rosie in Haughton, Sonny Benjamin in Perth and Maisie Ann in Kegworth. I think I had better get on and finish the book before it gets to look like a telephone directory!

Further footnote to my children: – Steven, Lee, and Michelle. Please stop now as it is starting to get expensive. If you need to, ring me and I can explain what is causing this population explosion and advise on methods of stopping it (a small fee may be involved).

Additional footnote. (This is getting boring now.) Do not read this book if you are of a nervous disposition or one of those politically correct, virtuous, snowflakes. I have never been politically correct and have even reached that age now that I do not care who I upset. If I end my days in prison for voicing my opinion, I will still not apologise for being me.

CHAPTER 1

THE DEAD SKELETON

Envisage, if you can, a public house, somewhere around the outskirts of London. This may be easier for some than for others, for reasons that will remain your own.

This establishment had a nightclub, which was still in use, attached to the main building via a corridor at the rear of the lounge. Very convenient to filter the clientele from the bar at closing time, suitably inebriated, to continue spending their hard-earned cash on more alcohol, at vastly inflated prices. Still, I suppose it kept them happy and provided further income for the staff and management.

As part of the refurbishment team, I was there doing the electrical work and was one of the very few who had access to the nightclub. This was in order to gain entry to the electrical switchgear in that part of the building. Hiding the key to the adjoining door was paramount as obviously the premises were full of alcohol and with anything up to thirty, thirsty, hungry, greedy, and unscrupulous vagabonds working on site it was down to me if anything went missing or got broken!

Occasionally somebody would request the key on the pretence that they needed the toilet as the one available was already occupied, and they were desperate, or some other nefarious reason. However, after being questioned about diminishing stocks behind the bar, on a couple of occasions, I became aware that I would have to accompany anyone who had a genuine reason to go in. Not actually accompany them into the toilet you understand, just around the vicinity! Honest,

3

your honour!

The refurbishment project was around the halfway mark when Halloween loomed on the horizon. The management of the nightclub had really made a grand effort to dress the premises of the nightclub up for the occasion, with scary spider's webs and ghosties and ghoulies (scary things, not men's appendages that is) hanging from all available areas.

At this point in time, I must stress, for people that have not worked in this sort of construction environment, that practical jokes and general wind ups are a constant hazard, and one always must be on the lookout.

At the centre of the stage, in the nightclub was a display that had, for its centrepiece, a life-sized inflated black and white skeleton hanging from a light fitting.

One day, in my wisdom, I decided to borrow said skeleton, in order to wind up one of the lads named Jimmy.

Now, Jimmy was a nice enough chap, for a painter and decorator anyway, but a little weird in some people's eyes. He was a definite lady's man – but with a difference. Every night when working away from home he would go to one of the hostelries local to where he was staying and look for a woman. Okay nothing strange about that, for men working away from home, you might think. Hence the extraordinarily high divorce rate amongst carpenters, electricians, plumbers etc. But no, not for Jimmy the average, blonde, lithe, pretty, take me home to meet your mum, sort of girl. Oh no, Jimmy looked for exceptionally large, fat, ugly, muscle-bound, tattooed, unkempt women. He insisted that they would not only take him to bed after buying him drinks all night but would be grateful as no one else would look twice at them. In his words 'They do not yell, they don't tell and they're grateful as hell.' He also insisted that as no one else would bother with them, he would not take any nasty diseases home

4

to his wife – at least none that he did not already have.

None of us could consider the sight of Jimmy, who incidentally was about five feet six inches high and weighed about six stone dripping wet, in the arms of a large, ugly, naked Amazonian. At least none of us wished to conjure up such a sight!

If Jimmy stood sideways and pulled out his tongue, he did a great impression of a trouser zip. One of the people in this world that needs to run around in the shower to get wet and stand twice in the same place to cast a shadow – I have a hatred for such people – I look at a Mars bar and I put three pounds on!

On this day, as was usual, all the lads on site were sat around having lunch. I decided this may be a suitable time to isolate a certain electrical circuit so as not to cause any inconvenience by removing the available lights whilst the lads were working (only electricians are considerate like that). This entailed entering the nightclub to gain access to the fuse board in there.

Upon seeing the skeleton, a fiendish thought entered my head. I carefully removed it, after making sure that none of the nightclub staff were present. Hugging the skeleton to my side I waltzed into the bar where the lads were chatting and announced that 'Jimmy' and I were going to go out looking for a 'Big Momma' to keep him warm tonight. Everybody fell about laughing, except the man at the centre of the joke, who sat poker faced, halfway through munching his sandwich.

'Come on Jimmy,' I said, as we made our way toward the outside door, unaware that behind me the real Jimmy had arisen from his seat, with evil intent firmly on his mind.

Slowly and silently, still amidst roars of laughter, Jimmy approached my rear (good job I was not a fat woman). As he came upon me and my 'friend' he pulled out of his overall pocket his large decorator's scissors and with one swift movement of said implement, cut the skeleton in half, right in the centre of its spine.

The laughter abruptly stopped and in the stillness a spider in the corner was heard to fart, before there were gasps of horror followed by ear shattering mirth. I stood there clutching a half-deflated lump of plastic whilst the other half lay slowly crumpling on the floor. Thoughts of retribution meted out by the nightclub staff, against me, flashed through my mind. A vision of my naked, bloodied, beaten corpse hanging from a certain light fitting, in place of the skeleton, in a nightclub not a million miles from where I stood, sped across my consciousness, as a nasty smell emanated from my underpants.

Whilst the rest of the crew continued to fall around laughing, I desperately searched my mind for a way out of the situation. I knew that I only had a couple of hours before the manager and some of the other staff turned up at the nightclub to fill the shelves and coolers ready for opening that night. I grabbed the shrivelled lumps of PVC and ran for the van, hoping in vain that I would be able to find a local shop where a replacement could be found. After around thirty minutes and numerous outlets in the vicinity it was obvious that nothing comparable was to be found and the general consensus of opinion was that it had come from America. This was in the days before Halloween became popular in England and truly little in the way of decorations was available locally unless by special order.

I did manage to buy a roll of clear tape however and set off back to the site.

Amidst much merriment and calls of things such as 'Where's your friend' and 'Jimmy has a bone to pick with you' I sat in the corner trying my best to affect a repair to the sad item. After about five attempts the limp body actually seemed to come back to life as I desperately re-inflated it. At this point I was thankful that the inflation point was at the rear of the head and not between the legs, as blowing in at this juncture would have surely invited more lewd and caustic comments!

I crept sheepishly back to the nightclub, uttering a sigh of relief as the place was still deserted. I then hung 'Jimmy' back in his rightful place, whilst uttering a silent prayer to whoever the patron saint of jokes is. I had no sooner stepped from the stage when John, the manager, came through the front door. After passing the time of day in a polite manner and hoping that he did not notice me sweating profusely – strange for a cool October afternoon – I returned to site hoping that nothing or nobody would feel 'let down' (pun fully intended) by my actions.

It seems that my efforts were not entirely in vain, as it was the beginning of the following week before John appeared in the bar, with Jimmy's counterpart, asking if anyone knew how 'he' came to be 'taped up'. Breaking out in a bath of perspiration I sat waiting for someone to point the finger in my direction, but everyone denied any knowledge and John returned to the nightclub, as I was reliably informed that I was buying at least the first two rounds of drinks that night for all the lads.

This episode just goes to show how easily things can backfire on the perpetrator, but then again will never stop similar things happening – as can be seen in the ensuing pages.

CHAPTER 2

THE STRIPPERGRAM

Salisbury has a wealth of lovely old buildings, not least of all The King's Arms. This hotel and public house located directly opposite Salisbury Cathedral, has some parts dating back hundreds of years and has been the scene of many acts of treachery, deceit, and trickery. None more so than when it underwent a major refurbishment in the 1980s!

It was a job that was scheduled to last for many weeks and cost many thousands of pounds and subsequently saw a large number of people passing through its portals. Very few were to escape the attentions of the vast number of practical jokers on site!

Due to the sheer number of men involved, we were residing in more than one location. Some had bed and breakfast accommodation in Salisbury but others, including myself, were in a small pub a few miles away in a little village called Bulford. As many people will be aware, it is also situated just down the road from a rather large army camp or was at the time. This was a lovely old establishment run by a very charming couple who were assisted by their sixteen-year-old daughter.

Almost every day on site someone was subject to the wit or maliciousness of someone else. There was a dearth of parking spaces available close by and this almost invariably meant leaving one's vehicle in the corporation car park some distance down the road. Unfortunately, this entailed it being out of sight, and more than one poor soul was summoned to the ground floor to try and explain that his car or van was not really for sale at a ridiculously cheap price, as revealed by the sign under the windscreen wipers. One rather large and ugly looking prospective purchaser, a member of the travelling community I believe, got quite irate after finding out that he could not buy a perfectly good Transit van for £150, and threatened all sorts of actions against the perpetrators of such a cruel joke. Unfortunately, or perhaps fortunately, he had no more idea than the rest of the lads on site, except the culprits that is, as to whom it was.

Being the boss of the electrical contracting company meant that I frequently had to attend the site meetings, held periodically in order to check on progress, and agree on any changes. These meetings were held in any room on site – anywhere that was available at that phase of the project.

Somebody, and I never discovered who, decided that I was to be the subject of the next jape and subsequently went around the site collecting money from everyone, in anticipation of the evil deed.

Come the day of the next site meeting and I was sitting there along with various other people, mostly in suits, shirts, and ties, including the project manager, the quantity surveyor and some of the top members of the breweries' staff. Obviously, I had to keep these people sweet in the hope of procuring further work in the future, always treating them with respect and keeping quiet unless my opinion was sought.

Unbeknown to me, a few miles away there was a young lady, dressed very scantily under her raincoat, preparing to be chauffeured to the site. Upon arrival at her destination, she discarded the raincoat to reveal a frilly basque, fishnet stockings and stiletto heels. Yes, the money had been invested in a strippergram. Now surely any red-blooded male, such as me, would welcome the opportunity to be held in the arms of this veritable mirage! Well, maybe not if he saw that the basque was straining to hold back around 152 kilograms of throbbing flesh! That is about twenty-four stone in old money for those of you that have still not gone metric. Yes, it was what I believe is termed a roly-poly-gram. Apparently, the cheeks of her backside hung down to her knees, when let loose, and if she sneezed it was usually recorded at about 4.2 on the Richter scale.

Only Jimmy would have enjoyed being enveloped in such a manner.

It did not matter where you were in the room – she was next to you! Her husband had at some time insisted that she had her ears pierced so that their kids could watch the television.

Now, being embraced by such a woman, dressed as she was and quivering like a gelatinous whale, would not exactly be the way to show the big-wigs – the same ones that I was desperate to impress – how dedicated I was to fulfil their every need.

As I sat there explaining why I required an open cheque, for the extra works that had been undertaken so far, the door opened and in stepped one of the painters. He looked straight at me as he apologised for the interruption. He then requested that someone's car be moved as it was in danger of being damaged. Meanwhile, the strippergram, preparing to cascade onto her unsuspecting victim, was asking where I was situated, as all the lads on site assembled outside the meeting, anxiously awaiting my near death by asphyxiation.

Now I do not believe in guardian angels, but that day somebody or something must have been looking over me, even as something else prepared to pour all over me like an overgrown jelly. But apparently, there were two pubs of the same name or remarkably similar in or around Salisbury and she had tipped up at the other one. Unable to find someone to molest and consequently collect her fee, the young lady went home sulking and crying into her more than adequate cleavage.

Obviously, I was unaware of anything happening – or not

happening, fortunately – as the complete site eventually drifted back to work feeling very let down. A truly narrow escape in anyone's book.

You may now be thinking that this is the end of this particular tale and a terrible anti-climax but bear with me as it is not that simple. My luck, although holding out so far, was not to continue too much longer.

We always put in a long, hard, day at work despite the frivolity involved on most days. Consequently, by the time we reached our accommodation, we were always ready for a shower or bath and a hard-earned pint or two (or as usual, considerably more) and something to eat. Fortunately for us, being accommodated in licensed premises, as we were, this was easy enough – except for the shower/bath. As there was only one bathroom to service around eight bedrooms, it was always a fight to reach it first. The alternatives were to work a little later or retire to the bar for a couple of dust settlers prior to washing and eating. Unfortunately, we were all too aware that the latter action sometimes turned into an absence, for the rest of the evening, of one or more of the others, as had been demonstrated many times in the past. Waking up the next morning still dressed in yesterday's clothes, stinking like an old eel, and nursing a hangover is not the best way to start the day! Many times, when not stopping in licensed premises, the tendency was to stop on the way back for *just one to settle the dust* and often ended in a doner kebab or fish and chips after being asked to vacate the premises as it was long past closing time.

Sensibly awaiting your turn often resulted in lying on the bed reading and listening for the sound of the bathroom door. The downside to this, if on your own in a bedroom, was often to wake in the early hours of the morning, hungry, thirsty, and still mucky – still you could almost guarantee the bathroom was vacant by then even if there was no hot water.

Anyway, to get back to the story, on this particular occasion I was not fortunate enough to avail myself of the bathroom until everyone else had showered or bathed. It seemed as if the entire workforce was determined to deny me a chance to be freshened up for my foray to the bar, by queuing up to take their turns. This, as often, meant a shower, or usually a wash down in water that was at best slightly warm, at worst freezing cold. Eventually, I had a wash and got changed and headed for the bar, gagging for suitable sustenance. As I walked into the bar room, all the lads, unusually, were crowded around the one end of the bar drinking and chatting. Suddenly a deathly silence prevailed, followed quickly after, by an outburst from an extremely irate landlord, who seemed intent on removing two intimate parts of my anatomy, in a very unorthodox manner, and feeding said items to his extremely large, ugly dog. The fact that the lads were holding down the bar hatch did not seem to deter him from his mission, as he jumped over the bar and chased me from the room. I fled out of the pub and up the road, totally and innocently unaware of what possible crime I could have committed in order to deserve such punishment being meted out to my beautiful body (beauty is in the eyes of the beholder, thank-you).

Fortunately for me, a stocky landlord that spent most of his time propping up a bar was no competition for a terrified electrician, doing an impression of a greyhound with his arse on fire, at the same time as returning to his childhood and wishing that he were still wearing a nappy to contain the mess emanating from his rear end.

After a while he gave up and returned, while I continued to pass the members of the local running club, training for the forthcoming Olympics. Unable to sustain this method of transport for too long, I collapsed in a heap by the side of the road and lay there panting like a woman giving birth to quintuplets.

For the next hour I lay there considering what heinous crime of which I was guilty. I had not wet the bed or piddled in the wardrobe (both of which I have known other workers to do whilst inebriated),

I had not screwed his wife or had drinks without paying or even used too much toilet paper whilst on the premises. I knew I was an innocent man (this time) and finally resolved to return and plead my case.

As I entered the bar, the landlord and his wife were nowhere to be seen. Serving the drinks instead, was their sixteen-year-old daughter who smiled surreptitiously at me as I furtively approached waving a scrap of white paper that I had picked up on the way. Upon finishing serving the previous customer she turned to me and smiled again, this time with a hint of gratitude and a look that almost conveyed pity.

'I do appreciate the gesture,' she said, 'but I am only sixteen and you are a good deal older – a fact not entirely lost by myself. And besides, I already have a boyfriend, who incidentally will be here shortly. By the way, did I mention he is from the army camp up the road, weighs seventeen stone, stands six feet four inches in his socks, and is built like a brick outhouse? Also, he is the extremely jealous type.'

By now I was totally dumbfounded as to what I had done, as the rest of the bar smirked into their drinks.

At this point in walked a group of squaddies headed by a particularly large guy, looking like King Kong who had just been told that he was grounded for a month with no pocket money. As the others blocked the only exit, he approached the bar asking, 'Okay where is he?'

As Maria pointed to me, I prepared to disappear up my own backside and drag it in after me, as he turned to me and asked what the idea was of sending flowers to his sixteen-year-old girlfriend?

Now I was totally confused and began to stutteringly appeal to his better nature, whilst licking his size thirteen army issue boots.

I really did not know any of what had gone on and was speechless when Maria produced a wonderful bouquet of flowers and showed them to me. Attached to the bouquet was a little card saying: -

'I fell for you the first time I saw you and cannot stop thinking of you. Please will you grant me the honour of going out to dinner with me? I really think we could be good together.

P.S. Please tell nobody else about this.'

As I stood there speechless, I glanced around, only to see the lads in the corner rolling around in fits of laughter. Looking back to Maria and the others, they could no longer contain themselves as the whole building seemed to shake with laughter.

It seems that the whole world was in on the joke – except me of course. Instead of giving everyone their money back from the whip-round, some plonker – and I never discovered who that was either – had come up with the idea of sending the bouquet, supposedly from me to Maria. After getting over the initial shock, of the human barrage balloon not turning up to the site meeting, they were all informed of what was going down and agreed to go along with it (isn't it great having mates?)

After changing my soiled underpants, we all settled down to a good drink and a meal to round off the night as my evil mind plotted its sordid revenge. I would have to really excel myself in the future to make someone pay for this one.

CHAPTER 3

THE GREAT FIRE OF SALISBURY

Just occasionally, even in such an innocuous place such as a building site, something occurs that proves the old adage of *The boy who cried "wolf"*. This happened whilst at the same site as before in Salisbury and very nearly ended in terrible disaster.

As usual, we were sat drinking, at about 10 o'clock one ordinary weeknight, when the landlord said that there was a telephone call for me. Wondering who on earth that could be at this hour I wandered over to the bar (a lot of wondering/wandering involved). Picking up the offered receiver, a familiar voice, who I identified straight away as the site foreman, informed me that the hotel that we had been working in earlier that day was on fire and could I go back into Salisbury and see what was happening.

Now, a twenty-minute ride into town at that time of night, under the influence of alcoholic substances, did not seem like a good idea. Plus, given the number of tricks played so far on site, and the fact that the project was coming toward the end, even in my inebriated state I was unlikely to fall for such a joke.

The conversation went something like, 'Yeah, yeah, you must think I came over on the last banana boat,' before I replaced the handset on its cradle. I went back to my pint before it got warm – or consumed by some burly Scotsman (it happens in London, I know, I was that soldier) – only to be forcibly dragged back to the telephone within seconds by the landlord, who by this time was also getting fed up.

'I'm not kidding,' stated John, 'it really is burning, and I have not got any transport to get to site as someone has borrowed my car.'

'Look,' said I, using my best authoritative voice, 'firstly, you are in town already, so a walk would obviously do you some good, given that you are suffering from alcohol induced hallucinations. Secondly, I personally have not drunk enough to douse a fire by piddling on it and thirdly I am not stupid enough to fall for your pathetic attempt at a wind-up. See you in the morning bright and early.' I duly hung up and returned once more to the serious task of rescuing my beer.

An alcohol induced sleep followed in order to awake the next morning bright eyed and bushy tailed (I wish). Following a good fried breakfast to soak up the beer we all toddled off to face whatever the day would throw at us.

As we rolled up at the site the following morning, we were more than a little surprised to see a fire engine in the road outside – surely even John had not got the influence to call up the fire service just to continue a joke.

Sure enough, as I walked in, I was greeted by the smell of smoke and a variety of glum faces. The fire had apparently been put out and I was informed that it had been isolated to one of the bedrooms on the top floor. Obviously today was going to be an enforced holiday as the fire service carried out an investigation. Unable to glean much information immediately, it was soon obvious that an adjournment to the nearest 'greasy spoon' was called for. Whilst drinking copious amounts of tea, speculation was rife as to the cause of the fire, the favourite theory being it was an electrical fault. Well, is that not just typical, blame the most innocent and vulnerable party?

Eventually, unable to take any more tea, everyone filtered back to their respective accommodations where more theories and speculations were chewed over with the assistance of a few comforting alcoholic beverages.

The following day, it transpired that the fire had been caused by a discarded cigarette end. Electricians exonerated! Apparently, it had started under the floor of the bedroom where the painters were storing all their equipment. Someone must have dropped a cigarette butt and it had rolled between the enormous oak planks. The same oak planks that had survived about six hundred years, before being accidentally sabotaged by some careless cretin wielding paintbrush bristles in place of their grey matter.

It was only purely due to luck that the fire was spotted in time. It turned out that the hotel manager, who lived just across the yard in a separate house, spotted a light that had been left on as he was going to bed. Deliberating if he should venture across and turn it off, he decided to do so before he and his wife retired for the night. As he climbed the stairs, he heard a noise coming from the top floor. Empty premises... 600 years old... late at night... strange noises...shivers running down his spine...an empty feeling in his heart and butterflies the size of ostriches in his stomach, he swallowed his fear and had the foresight to investigate.

As he entered the top corridor, by torchlight, he could just make out smoke emanating from under the door of a bedroom, accompanied by a dull glow...if this were a ghost then he was definitely arson about. Realizing that a slice of Salisbury's rich history was at stake he flew down the stairs, pyjamas flapping almost as much as he was, shouting 'Fire, Fire', desperate to reach a telephone before the building was engulfed before his very eyes.

Fortunately, the fire brigade turned up within a few minutes and successfully doused the flames, although at the cost of water damage to a vast portion of the partially refurbished rooms.

We were reliably informed by the fire chief that another five minutes could have been the end of the building, as tins of highly inflammable paint stripper and paint had swelled to bursting point. If they had burst and ignited, then the chances of putting out the inferno that ensued would have been very slim indeed.

The consequences were long reaching. The fire and smoke damage to that bedroom and the water damage to the floors below were horrendous.

Days and nights were spent on site attempting to bring the project back on schedule. The alcohol was replaced by caffeine tablets as the hours and days melted into one. Most of the bodies were only kept going by the thought of all the extra money being doled out by some insurance company.

By some miracle of fortitude, the hotel re-opened its doors on time after some amazing dedication to the cause, and the thought of a solid week of drinking, eating, and sleeping that awaited at the end of an exceptionally long tunnel.

The cry of 'wolf' was soon forgotten as life returned to *'normal'*.

CHAPTER 4

'POETS' Day

Of course, life on site was not all frivolity and happiness. Sometimes bad things lurked around the corner and often disaster struck at the most inopportune moments – otherwise known as *'Shit Happens'.*

Whilst working away from home most of the guys looked forward to POETS Day After enduring a strange bed – never the best beds in cheap accommodation – and basic living for a week or two at a time, coupled with the danger of alcoholic poisoning, Friday was a day to behold. To return to a loving home where creature comforts were easily taken for granted and a comfortable bed was calling was considered heavenly. To sit on one's own toilet with a good book and not have three or four blokes hammering on the door and screaming abuse was utter bliss. To survive two days without eating a kebab, that under normal circumstances you would not feed to a dog, was as good as it gets.

To be honest, some of the bed and breakfast establishments we have stayed in over the years would have been rejected by the homeless. Nobody minded too much finding a dead flea in their bed – it was the other thousand that had come to its funeral that was the problem. The normal procedure in a new place was to pull back the bedclothes with the left hand and immediately dab all over the bottom sheet with a sticky bar of soap, then examine whatever had not managed to escape. To be fair not all were like this, but if you were late arriving and had to have what was left, life could be rougher than camping out in the Amazonian rainforest for the week, with just a bin liner for protection.

As Friday usually entailed travelling home, often from London, up a remarkably busy M1, it was prudent to make an early getaway if at all possible. Things became so bad in latter years that if you were not on the road home by about two o'clock Friday afternoon, then you knew that you were lucky to get home within four hours, and if there was an accident, as often happened, this would be considerably longer.

Consequently, Friday was referred to on site as POETS Day which stood for – 'Push Off Early, Tomorrow's Saturday' – although the word push was usually substituted on site by a more basic word for urination.

Sometimes this was easier said than done though and a classic case comes to mind. Lenny and Ben had been away in London for two straight weeks and were desperate to return home to the Midlands and their loved ones. Thursday night was a night for celebration and a few pints were in order before returning to their wives and families the following day.

Donning their best togs, or the best that they were allowed to take away with them, they headed to the local hostelry for a bar meal and something to wash it down.

Being painters and decorators, they were brought in towards the end of the contract and had worked long hours that fortnight to ensure that their side of the project was ahead of schedule. After a nice relaxing weekend, a steady time the following week would ensure the job was 'put to bed' on time.

Unfortunately, the job was not the only thing 'put to bed' that night.

Around nine thirty, two very nice-looking young ladies approached the bar. Immediately, Ben was off the starting blocks like a cheetah after a gazelle.

'Can I buy you ladies a drink?' said Ben, with about as much subtlety as a navvy using a jackhammer to crack a walnut. As the one girl turned to her mate and smiled, Ben turned to Lenny and winked. The girls joined the boys at their table, chatting amiably. By closing time, much money had been passed across the bar and the hangovers were rubbing their hands, ready for an early start the next morning.

'Want to come back to the digs for a night cap?' slurred Lenny to Mary, the blonde girl sitting next to him. After some discussion, and Jane phoning a friend, the four of them made their way back to the guest house and as quietly as possible, in their inebriated condition, climbed the stairs to one of the lad's rooms. Although it was slightly more expensive, they always had single rooms due to Lenny's tendency to snore like a rhinoceros on heat.

Lenny really had 'the hots' for Mary but unfortunately Mary had designs on Ben. Following a girlie get together in the toilet next door, the girls returned to the bedroom and announced that they would only stay for a while if Mary could effectively swap partners.

Ben and Mary disappeared to Ben's room whilst a sulky and dejected Lenny sat talking to Jane. Although Lenny and Jane eventually ended up in bed together, the excessive drink took over them both and they fell sound asleep.

As the night wore on Jane awoke with a start fearing that another chainsaw massacre was about to take place. Sitting up in bed she realised that the noise was emanating from the mouth of the body lying comatose next to her. Three digs in the ribs and a glance at the clock later convinced her that it was time to head for home.

Placing a pillow over Lenny's head, Jane switched on the light and proceeded to get dressed. With the sound of the timber yard saw still running in the bed she crept next door to rouse Mary. Explaining it was time to go, Jane passed Mary's clothes and waited whilst she dressed and led the way out of the building and down the road to the nearest bus stop.

At eight o'clock the alarm inside Lenny's head was still thumping as Ben entered his room.

'Have a look at my back Lenny will you,' said Ben 'it feels very sore. I don't know what I have done.'

As he lifted his shirt and turned around, Lenny let out a cry at the claw marks raked down Ben's shoulders and back.

'Oh shit,' gasped Lenny 'your back looks like a busy road map. You must have been pretty drunk not to feel that happening.'

At the same time, he could not help thinking to himself, *'Hell that could have been me.'*

Immediately after breakfast, a trip to the pharmacy and a generous application of antiseptic cream were in order.

Although the stinging on his back subsided, the nagging in Ben's brain that he could not possibly go home that day persisted.

'Lenny, you go home, and I will stay here,' said Ben. 'There is no way I can let Margaret see my back and I know I will not be able to hide it all weekend. I will have to ring her and tell her that I have had to stay and do some extra work.'

Lenny duly obliged and made the long journey home alone, constantly thanking the guardian angel that was looking over him.

Meanwhile, Ben rang Margaret and explained about the extra work that had arisen and the need to stay until the following weekend. This was not an altogether unique situation and did not ring any alarm bells with Margaret.

The following day, Beth, Lenny's wife, decided to go to the supermarket and obviously it was necessary to take hubby along as they had not seen each other all week. And anyway, she needed someone to carry the shopping (sound familiar lads?) and to pay for it. Along they went to the local shopping centre where Beth begrudgingly dragged Lenny around almost every shop in order to satisfy her need for some 'retail therapy'. Lenny did little protesting as all he could think of was Ben, sitting in the bedroom in London, feeling deeply sorry for himself and practising contortionism in order to apply cream to unreachable parts of his anatomy.

All was going well until they reached the wine and spirits section in the supermarket. As Lenny and Beth rounded the corner, Lenny's eyes made immediate contact with Margaret's, who was coming in the opposite direction. At that moment he could feel the surprise and suspicion boring into his brain and knew that the only 'porky pies' he would experience that day were the ones he had to tell the two women who were about to envelop him in explanations, excuses, and downright lies.

Beth, unknowingly, set the stage, by enquiring why Margaret had allowed Ben to escape the 'honour' of being dragged screaming and kicking around the shops instead of playing golf or putting his feet up in front of the television. Little known to them, Ben was indeed lay on his bed watching television, the site was closed for the weekend, and he had neither the funds nor the desire to go out getting inebriated.

Margaret suspiciously looked at Lenny whilst explaining to Beth that Ben was still stuck in London, doing extra work that had cropped up and would not be home until next weekend. Both women turned to Lenny, who at that moment in time wished he had the ability to crawl up his own backside and drag it in after him.

As his mind raced, he was aware of a stereophonic bleating about why he was here in the supermarket whilst Ben was in London.

Eventually, as he was allowed to squeeze a word in edgeways, he explained that there was only enough work to keep one person busy over the weekend, and he and Ben had flipped a coin to see who would have to stay and who would go home. This appeared to appease the two women, although Lenny could not help feeling that Margaret's glare was focussed on him and felt compelled to turn his attention to the vast array of beers on display whilst Margaret and Beth put the rest of the world to rights.

It was not until Lenny returned to London the following Monday morning, he learned of the grief that Margaret had inflicted upon his friend over the telephone.

The next weekend came around all too quickly and despite numerous applications of ointment, some of the marks on Ben's back were still discernible. Obviously staying a further weekend was definitely not an option. Ben and Lenny returned home that weekend and Ben's attempts to keep his back concealed were successful right up until Monday morning.

Lenny's mobile rang bright and early and as soon as he answered, he could tell by Ben's tone that something was amiss. Ben only said that he would not be returning to London that day as he had 'a few things to sort out' and he would catch the train down, probably the next day.

As it transpired, Ben arrived on site Wednesday afternoon, wearing a face like a smacked arse. The ensuing divorce was swift, messy, and expensive. Both men fought and lied hard to keep Lenny from being implicated and suffering a similar fate, although Beth's suspicions were far from allayed and inspections of all parts of his anatomy were soon the order of the day upon arriving home after a hard week away from home.

I am sure there are lots of lads in various trades that can fully empathise with what occurred. There but for the grace of a few scratches go many of you.

CHAPTER 5

'POETS' Day – 2

The next adventure recalled, entailed a job in Chatham in Kent. I was employed by a company that installed fire alarm and nurse call systems at the time and this obviously entailed working in hospitals and nursing homes, all around the country, a lot of the time.

This job was to install a new fire alarm system at All Saints Hospital in Chatham. It has probably changed a lot since then – at least I hope it has, for the patient's sakes – but at the time consisted of a whole bunch of dark, damp Dickensian buildings spread out over a large site. Just to fetch materials from our store would usually involve a considerable walk, but fortunately it also meant passing the canteen, so a cup of tea and a chat to the girls behind the counter usually made it worthwhile.

After a week of working in such an establishment, Friday was a day to embrace religiously.

Let me tell anyone that has not worked in environs that are all female, that it is usually worse than a building site full of navvies. Many are the times I have been working below the desks or in cupboards inside offices occupied solely by women and the conversation have turned to women's opinions and thoughts regarding men and sex etc. Out of sight, out of mind, under the desks, often is the occasion I have had to crawl away into a corner or some other refuge to escape the embarrassment. Let me say now that I am a man of the world and do not get embarrassed easily, but, when the talk gets that explicit, I have been known to cringe slightly.

A lot of women in the maternity departments seem to lose their inhibitions completely – I have since had a couple of spells in hospital myself (no, not the maternity) and know that when you enter hospital as a patient, you have to leave your modesty on the welcome mat – and the comments received, when working in or walking through these wards, was sometimes frightening to a young man, in the prime of his life, with raging hormones, and away from his nuptial bed.

Coupled with working in departments such as the psychiatry and children's wards it is little wonder that Friday could not come soon enough

All this is apart from looking through a hole in the ceiling one day, only to see a body being dissected in the pathology department. Fascinating, but a little gruesome and I do admit to being fussy in the canteen at lunchtime that day. I definitely would not have liver and onions or steak and kidney pie.

Anyway, to get back to the story, one Friday, well into the contract, we decided, following a particularly productive week, to hit the road by lunchtime in order to give us a head start on the traffic. This is in the days before the M25 existed (yes, I really am that old) and therefore the journey from the M1 motorway across country to Chatham took a considerable time – especially in an old, clapped-out Mark 2 Ford Cortina that had once suffered the humiliation of being overtaken, uphill, by an electric milk float.

So off we set, across Kent and subsequent counties and towns on our way to the M1 motorway. Prior to hitting the M1 there is, or was at the time, a long stretch of dual carriageway which signalled that the journey to the motorway was soon to be on its final leg.

About three miles before we reached the M1, Steve, who was working with me at the time, shouted 'there's John.'

'Where?' asked I in a desperate panic.

'On the other side, going towards site.'

'Are you sure?'

'Absolutely!'

Steve was a nice, reliable sort of fellow, and like me was not fond of the idea of losing his job for absconding early on a Friday.

John, on the other hand was the company foreman, or should I say, 'camp commandant' and Hitler stand-in. He ruled with a fist of iron and just adored catching workers disobeying his orders. He had made it obvious, in previous weeks, that he suspected Steve and I of slacking our duty (bloody cheek), and indeed had even turned up on site at 08:00 on the Tuesday morning the week before to attempt to catch us being late. Fate had smiled upon us that day as the landlady's husband had informed us that she was unwell and would be unable to get us breakfast that day. Subsequently we had turned up on site early and was on our way to the hospital canteen, to indulge in a nice 'full English', when 'Obersturmbahnfuhrer' John popped up out of the woodwork.

Thanks again, guardian angel.

Careful Alec, I might get to take up religion at this rate. Do not get me wrong, I did attend church regularly at this time of my life – mainly because they had a good pool table at the Church Tavern!

So, as it was a dual carriageway, we had no option but to carry on to the next roundabout before doing an about turn and putting the pedal to the metal with the intention of returning to site as quickly as possible in the rustmobile. The countryside rushed by in a veritable blur as the clone of Noddy's auto cruised at top speed (almost touching the dizzy heights of 60mph) whilst panic set deeper and deeper into our black souls.

Steve suddenly said, 'I know, ring John, and see where he is. That will confirm if I was right or not.'

27

'Great idea Steve,' said I 'but if he is on the way to site and given the fact that he is sure to arrive before us, it will only make him suspicious when he is unable to find us.'

'Yeah, never thought of that,' Steve replied.

Silence overtook us as we struggled to think of a way to avoid the prospect of a P45 – neither of us had a birthday imminent and so did not want our cards.

I vowed to myself that I would never be caught out again in such a situation, and that I would also polish the car the coming weekend, to a brilliant shine, to attempt to increase the aerodynamics and gain extra speed.

Onward we sped, eating up the miles (and the petrol) as the prospect of an early day disappeared.

Eventually we arrived back at site armed with a story of nipping into town to fetch some required part or other. Parking up in our usual spot we hurried to open our storeroom and put on the company overalls ready to be taken to our leader.

Checking all parts of the hospital was a considerable undertaking (especially the mortuary – undertaking yeah! Oh, please yourself!) but one that we undertook with alacrity. Eventually after searching high and low for the exalted one, we retired to the canteen for a cup of tea and a change of plan. The girls in the canteen agreed that they had not set eyes on John either, as Steve attempted to crawl under the tables to avoid a severe beating from me.

We rang the office and spoke to John, on the premise of needing some materials the following week, before setting off for home again.

Weary and bedraggled after sitting in various traffic jams I dropped Steve off outside his house. In hindsight I suppose I should have stopped the car whilst doing so but I was anxious to get home before her indoors went out on her broomstick for the night.

It just goes to show how it does not always pay being a little dishonest, our beer money for the following week severely depleted, after the extra petrol was taken out.

Oh well, we live and learn. Or do we?

CHAPTER 6

THE 'LADIES? OF THE NIGHT'

Bed and breakfast took up a lot of money over the weeks, and months, that a job ran for and therefore when the opportunity arose, a cheaper, if more basic, alternative was grasped with both hands.

Just such an occasion arose at a public house, that myself and some other lads were working at in the south of London. A total refurbishment was to be carried out and as it was an extremely large building, comprising bars, lounges, a restaurant, and function rooms, apart from accommodation and offices this was going to take a lot of months as opposed to weeks. Extending over five floors, including the extensive cellar areas, it was the sort of building where a map was needed for the first couple of weeks to ensure the trip home on Friday was a certainty.

One of the labourers went missing for three days before he eventually crawled across the bar, emaciated and hypothermic, having been lost in the labyrinth of rooms. This did not come as a surprise to many on site as his nickname was 'Bungalow'. He was granted this moniker as he had nothing up top. Bless him, he seemed quite proud to have gained a name that meant something, even if it was slightly derogatory.

As the building was so large, the refurbishment was to be carried out in phases, and this meant that the top floors would not be touched for many weeks to come. Money was always at a premium, especially being self-employed, so permission was sought to set up camp on the top floor. As it was infinitely cheaper than employing a security firm, the project manager was only too happy to have a live-in caretaker and security guard. The area that the 'pub' was in was not the most affluent place and indeed it was said that there was a waiting list to be mugged locally. Before its closure, the clientele was a select bunch and popular opinion was that most nights they were so drunk that they ended up fighting on the floor as no one was, by this time, capable of standing up straight. Being frightened of my own shadow in such a large, empty, desolate, haunted environment had to be weighed up against how much money was to be saved – it really was no contest, and therefore I became the keeper of the keys.

There were downsides to this situation of course. I had to be up in time to let the first workers in, who started at 7 a.m. to beat the London traffic. Meals were cooked on a single burner camping stove meaning camp stew was usual. Washing in cold water was kept to a minimum after lifting off the sheet of ice, and a beard became a necessary part of life. I became accustomed to working alone on site – possibly due to my unkempt and unwashed appearance. Indeed, the situation became so bad that one time, when going to the shop down the road for provisions, I was stopped by an old boy in rags, clutching a bottle in a brown paper bag, who offered to give me money if I would move to another street as I was bad for his begging business.

Over a couple of weeks, I managed to sort out a blow-up bed, sleeping bag, pillow and blankets and relative luxury was enjoyed. After all, the number of times I had slept in the front of the van or on an office floor were numerous by now, so I was quite easily pleased (oh, the joys of being self-employed).

I took a lot of ribbing on site about being tight but after a few weeks of paying out for digs, the heating engineers, as they insisted on being known as, (plumbers really) asked if they could move in with me. Being an affable sort of a chap, I agreed to a flexible lease on some floor space and drew up a set of rules that were to be adhered to. Truth be known, I was only too happy to have some company – at least noises in the night could be accounted for in future. I was by now almost used to being waken in the middle of the night by eerie sounds ensuring the lack of a need for laxatives, but also needing the regular washing out of underpants. The following week my new roommates Dave and Jock moved in.

Nice guys – Dave, English, married with two children, a mortgage, an affinity for football, a car, and a fairly 'normal' lifestyle – Jock, Glaswegian, single with four children – the ones that he owned up to anyway, no mortgage, an obsession with his local football club – including the before and after match fights, no car and a heavy drinker who told me that he had once nailed a guy's legs to the floor for molesting his sister. He said his prison sentence was worth every minute. I always tried extremely hard to keep in Jock's good books after that conversation.

We all got on very well and as the project progressed, we all three became good working and drinking buddies, although Dave and I never attempted to keep up with Jock as regards the drinking. The guy was like a sponge, the way he poured beer down his throat.

The rate that the job was going at meant Dave was forced to increase his labour force temporarily at one time and he appeared one Monday morning with Terry in tow alongside Jock.

Terry seemed like a decent enough sort of chap. Broke, and desperate to earn a few quid, he laboured away day after day and drank night after night – almost keeping up with Jock at times. After about four weeks he seemed to have earned enough to eventually be able to not have to borrow from everyone on site all week before paying out most of his wages on a Friday. The local bookie shop had apparently helped to boost his income after a good day of betting on the horses. Due to his financial constraints, Terry was still sleeping on the bare floorboards, as opposed to the mixture of inflatable beds, mattresses etc. that was strewed around our 'bedroom', but he seemed oblivious to the discomfort after his nightly lager style anaesthetic.

By now the work had progressed to such a rate that we found ourselves on site for two weeks at a time, before venturing home for a weekend in which to relax, bathe and generally freshen up ready for the next stint.

It was at about this time that I was asked, by the main contractor, if I could carry out a small job in the centre of London for them. The only problem was, it was in a bar and could only be started once the place was empty after about 11 o'clock on the night. Being a father of three – and a greedy, money grabbing little gobshite – I readily agreed. Arrangements were duly made and off I ventured one night into the big smoke with my trusty toolbox.

Fortunately, it was only a relatively small job and four in the morning saw me winging my way back to my much-needed bed.

Upon my arrival, being a thoroughly decent sort of a chap, I slipped off my boots and crept stealthily up the stairs and into the bedroom. Avoiding putting on the light for fear of waking someone – especially Jock – I carefully negotiated the path to my corner of the room. I was aware of slight muffled sounds coming from the far side of the room but just put it down to someone's version of snoring. After all, when you have spent years in different bedrooms with strange persons – and some of them can be strange – you get used to hearing the various melodious musings of inebriated bodies belching, farting, and snoring.

Ignoring the sounds, I undressed to my underpants (I always kept them on in case of emergency) and slid wearily into my sleeping bag.

My weariness disappeared as I realised that my sleeping bag was not there, as neither was my inflatable bed or insulating blanket and I was actually laying on the bare floorboards, a position not too comfortable and with the possibility of resulting in a likelihood of getting splinters in a rather delicate portion of my anatomy. Let us face facts at this juncture, you would certainly find out who your real friends are when it comes to removing splinters from your arse cheeks. I reached across to the far side of where my bed normally lay and grasped the torch that was kept there in the eventuality of it being needed in the middle of the night.

Scanning the room, by subdued torchlight, I could see that the chairs we kept for sitting on to eat our meals were arranged around Terry's bedding position with my blanket draped over them. I stood up and made my way across the room, intent on retrieving my possessions and intrigued by the makeshift tent. Terry had obviously 'borrowed' them, thinking that I would be away all night and he could indulge in some relative luxury for one night. Although why he needed to make a camp instead of using the blanket to lie on was beyond my comprehension.

As I came around the chairs, all I could see, in the weak torchlight, was a rather naked, pink bottom rising and falling. Not a pretty sight, believe me, in fact to tell the truth, it had a rather nasty crack in it. Quickly running the torch upwards and onwards I was met with a sight that I certainly was not expecting. There in the beam of the torch, lay a woman whose face resembled a bag of frogs, obviously intent on laying back and thinking of England whilst being pounded by an inebriated stud, trying for a place in the sex Olympics.

I am not quite sure what went through her head at that second, but I do know that she let forth a blood curdling scream, at the same time as bucking Terry face first onto the floor, where he carried on regardless making love to the floorboards. She lay there, naked as the day she was born (I tried not to look – honest) while Dave and Jock shot up in their respective beds, both shouting 'What the fuck is going on?' in perfect unison before Dave switched on the light and all was revealed – quite literally.

After the 'lady' had dressed herself, as we 'gentlemen' looked the other way, it was decided that a cup of tea (the good old English cure all) and an explanation may well be in order. As soon as Terry had finished being occupied with a knothole in the floorboards, the five of us sat around and drank a much-needed cup of tea as Dave, Jock and I listened to the saga that was unfolding from Terry and Julia. Julia being the nom-de-plume that she was owning up to on that night.

Apparently, Terry was feeling a little flush and after being broke for so long and leaving Dave and Jock in the local hostelry announced that he was going to catch the underground train into London and go to a club. The 'club' apparently turned out to be a seedy little joint in the heart of Soho, where ladies remove their clothes on the stage whilst gyrating in a seductive manner – or so I have been told – obviously, I never frequented such places myself. Julia, as she insisted was her name, worked in this club along with others and encouraged the clients to buy her champagne. As Terry was already quite drunk by the time, he reached these premises, a hand on his leg and a flash of stocking top was enough to procure the first bottle. After the second bottle of liquid gold, Terry had agreed to pay the stipulated fee and take Julia to *'His pad in the suburbs'* for a good time.

Although Terry's *'pad'* turned out to be a little less than the described 'Des. Res.', Julia had been paid, and agreed to make him a happy boy, on the premise that it was too late to return and con another punter anyway.

As Terry had passed out in a stupor by this time, Julia decided it was time to take her leave, but insisted that Terry had promised to provide the taxi fare back for her.

All three of us lads were unwilling to go through Terry's pockets as we were not quite sure what may be lurking in the corners of them – probably a half eaten sweet, a conker and a packet of contraceptives – so we had a whip round (I got ten lashes, the others twelve apiece) and Julia went on her way. Look, it is my story, and I can tell it how I want to.

I retrieved my bedding, and after inspecting it carefully, the three of us salvaged what was left of the night's rest.

The following morning, with Terry still in his coma and me, deservedly, lying in until break time, Dave agreed to unlock the site and let in the rest of the lads. At breakfast time, we awoke Terry, who insisted that someone was drilling holes inside his head, and his mouth resembled the bottom of a parrot's cage. Between us we recalled the night before, as we had encountered it. Terry could not remember much, if any, of it – what a waste of money it appeared.

Terry, upon checking his pockets, discovered that all his money had disappeared, along with the half eaten sweet, which he desperately needed at that juncture in time. He swore that he had had about four hundred pounds on his person when he had left work that night, which included his money for beer and meals the following week. I felt quite embarrassed as he described Julia in words that even I had not heard before. This tirade included, amongst other profanities, something about having a collection for her parents when they decide to get married.

He insisted that he would go back up to Soho that night and find her in order to retrieve his 'stolen' money. We managed to convince him that that would be a foolish thing to do, as he would undoubtedly end up in hospital – or the morgue, following a meeting with her pimp and the bouncers at the club. And anyway, he was totally bereft of funds and indeed owed us three for Julia's cab fare. This was before he would almost certainly be borrowing more during the coming week for the simple necessities of life, such as food and beer.

It was certainly a lesson hard learnt and it took a good long while for Terry to be feeling 'flush' again, as apart from the other expenses incurred that week, he also had to pay for my sleeping bag and blanket to be laundered. After all, something had to be done, in a desperate attempt to erase the memory of that bum – white as alabaster and cracked down the middle, rising and falling in the torchlight like a giant yo-yo. Yuk!

CHAPTER 7

THINGS THAT GO BUMP IN THE NIGHT!

I can also recall numerous other occasions when a good night's sleep has been interrupted for one reason or another.

None more so than in Paddington, London, when the bedroom was occupied by four of us hairy arsed male contractors. All in separate beds, I hasten to add. Not an ideal situation but financial restraints dictated that the more occupants to a bedroom, the cheaper the price. We all knew one another well enough to trust each other.

One of the occupants, a plumber by trade, was the main offender. He had asked if he could share a bedroom with us and unknowing of what lay in store, we readily agreed in order to make up the numbers. We were to discover that he never actually went to sleep at night. Instead, he would enter a comatose state that ensured a sprightly start – for him at least – the next morning. Unfortunately for the rest of us, as soon as he entered this dream world of nubile, scantily dressed, female plumbers – especially if he had been drinking, which was ninety-nine point nine per cent of nights – he would begin snoring. No, on second thoughts, it could not be classed as snoring. Obviously, I had heard people snoring before, but this was far and beyond any earthly, human noise.

It resembled someone using a jack hammer, on a concrete block, in the middle of a busy timber yard, where whole tree trunks were being sawn in half, whilst ZZ Top and Black Sabbath belted out a tune at peak volume. I am talking 'LOUD AND DEVASTATING'

Such a symphony of sound would surely equate to at least 6.9 on the Richter scale.

The first night someone threw a pillow at him, which caused a slight hiatus, but it soon resumed with renewed alacrity. Someone else threw a boot, someone else an ashtray, some one else a coin. Nothing seemed to work for long and the whole night was spent throwing and retrieving various items, shoving, or poking the offender's body, or shouting profanities, all in a vain attempt to gain some much-needed sleep before the dawn heralded another day of arduous toil.

As the morning light filtered through the grimy curtains, that attempted to fit the window opening, an amazing sight befell the eyes of us that were blearily able to focus. There on the fourth bed was a veritable mountain of clothes, boots, books, and other miscellaneous objects including a table, a chair, and a toilet seat – where that came from, I am not sure. The general consensus of opinion was that perhaps the plumber in question had decided to make an early start and had accumulated the detritus on his bed during a period of kleptomanic sleepwalking. BUT NO!

During the ensuing relative silence, as we stared at the apparition before us, a noise could be heard emanating from beneath the mountain of objects. We all three looked at each other, not really believing that a motorbike was inside the rubbish dump on the bed, even though it could clearly be heard revving up and then spluttering to a halt as though it had run out of fuel. But evidently it was not a motorbike, as at first thought, as a certain plumber's head appeared through the devastation, like a volcanic eruption, spewing forth a fountain of lava.

'Morning everyone,' the little voice piped up, 'looks like being another nice day. Did everybody sleep OK, I had a lovely night!'

At this point the revving of the motorbike was replaced with moans and groans, as three burly workmen descended on top of one confused plumber and began pummelling at whatever body parts could be reached in order to facilitate the removal of his (very) vocal cords, alongside other unmentionable parts of his anatomy.

It was noted that although the future brought about a need for the men to attempt to avoid being in the same bedroom as him, it was almost impossible not to hear him through the thin walls of cheap bed and breakfast establishments. It was rumoured that the share prices of certain pharmaceutical companies rose sharply in the ensuing weeks, as the sale of ear defenders and cotton wool went through the roof.

*

Sometimes, usually again because of financial restraints, you were forced to share a bedroom with other undesirable creatures.

Such an apparition was 'BIG MICK'. Standing about six feet, four inches tall and built like the proverbial brick s**t house, Mick's head consisted of a massive shock of long, curly, bright ginger steel wool. He looked like a cross between Herman Munster and Shirley Temple – the sort of sight to give children – and indeed most adults as well, the most horrendous nightmares. Toting him around on Halloween would have resulted in plenty of sweets, as people would surely have fled, leaving behind all their worldly possessions.

Every night whilst working away from home, Mick would frequent Indian, Bangladeshi, or other restaurants of similar persuasion. Once inside, he would order the hottest dish that the chefs could produce. Upon tasting it, he would then complain that it was not hot enough and comments like, 'Has this been in the fridge?' were met with utter disbelief by the management and staff, as well as by anyone daft enough to accompany him to eat.

I can remember when one of his fellow diners was stupid enough to taste a miniscule amount on the tip of a teaspoon. Despite drinking around four gallons of best tap water, later followed by a similar amount of lager, the hole in his tongue was clearly visible the next morning along with eyes that were streaming like mountain waterfalls.

I have even seen establishments where all the kitchen staff have appeared from the kitchen on the second night of patronage, to watch Mick attempt the 'uneatable dish' produced especially for him, only to be standing with chins on the floor, as he wolfed it down and complained once more about the lack of heat and spiciness. The man was truly an animal of uniqueness.

As if it was obligatory, this was always washed down with copious amounts of lager and the smoking of a couple of cigarettes. This was in the days when smoking was allowed anywhere and everywhere and a good night out necessitated placing all clothes worn that night into the weekly wash, bathing totally submerged for long periods of time and shaving off all bodily hair in order to remove the nicotine – and we called them the good old days!

By this time, I had quit smoking myself and I know that there is nothing worse than a reformed smoker to candidly point out what a dirty, filthy, despicable, unsociable, smelly habit it is. Everyone agreed unanimously, until such time as I walked off with my soap box. At this point they would all produce a packet and light up – even the non-smokers, who were fed up with hearing me go on about it.

Mick, in particular, smoked as though they were going out of fashion. In fact, it was rumoured that the Shirley Temple coiffure was only there to hide the chimney pot that sprouted from the top of his head.

On one occasion, four of us lads, including Mick were residing in a bedroom on the top floor of a bed and breakfast establishment in South London and Mick was, as usual, partaking of his usual evening sustenance regularly.

The morning routine, upon awakening usually consisted of the inevitable race to the bathroom, followed by the emergency opening of all portals by the unfortunate ones left. This was as much to escape the company of three other bodies that had eaten and drunk badly the night before, as to gain the relief of emptying one's bladder. You can only imagine the dawn chorus of belches alongside the smell of sweaty bodies, curry and lager farts and underwear that would have stuck to the wall if thrown.

It was during one of these morning sprints that I happened to glance at Mick as I passed his bed (not a sight to be recommended for anyone of a nervous or bilious disposition) only to spy a large gaping hole adjacent to his face. Thinking it was only Mick yawning I carried on toward the bathroom, glad to be out of the contaminated zone, where any fly unfortunate enough to be trapped would be seen doing an impression of Chris Tarrant or Sally James (those of you not old enough or not familiar with British Saturday morning television will have to consult someone of more senior years regarding *Tiswas* and *O.T.T.*).

Whilst carrying out my morning ablutions, a fleeting glimpse of Mick's head kept creeping through my mind, and I convinced myself to take a closer look on the way back – fortunately, I have a cast iron constitution after many years of sharing bedrooms with strange men (purely platonic and on a professional basis you understand).

Upon entering the bedroom, where all the other three were still ensconced in their stinking pits dreaming of their partners or other pretty girls – except Mick who was probably dreaming of chicken vindaloo with extra chillies, washed down with ten pints of the local brew – I glanced at Mick's pillow. Instead of the usual grubby, off-white, age encrusted sheen of the pillowcase, there, adjacent to the impression of a large ginger sheep was a large soot encrusted hole. It was patently obvious that Mick had awoken in the night, lit a cigarette, and then in a drunken, curry induced state, drifted off to sleep again without extinguishing it.

It was at about this point that I realised that, not only were we four floors up in a bedroom with no fire escape, and only six feet adjacent to Mick's bed, but there was no fire alarm or smoke detectors in the establishment either.

Upon informing the others of the situation, Mick was given a severe beating whilst still in his bed. He was also made to swear – on his copy of the Indian restaurant take-away menu – never to smoke in the bedroom again, at the risk of being held down and his curly locks forcibly removed one by one with pliers.

Fortunately, I am still here to tell the tale. It could so easily have ended in tragedy and was uncannily around the same time as the big fire at King's Cross Station, which was also caused by a cigarette, although I am happy to say that Mick was not to blame this time.

CHAPTER 8

HELD AT GUNPOINT!

Sometime during the 1970s – at the height of *'the troubles'* in Northern Ireland – we were carrying out a refurbishment project in London, at what at that time, was the offices of The Northern Ireland Tourist Board. The same building was also occupied by some other department from Northern Ireland to do with the commercial aspect of the country.

As time went on, more and more extra jobs were found and piled onto the contractor's workload. As extra works were always well paid this was a welcome bonus, but the downside was that the job was still expected to be finished on the original finishing date. Obviously, there are only twenty-four hours in any day and so it was inevitable that some weekend working would be required sooner or later.

Due to the fact that anything to do with Northern Ireland was of a sensitive nature at that time, special dispensation had to be sought to work at any time that was out of normal office hours. This was applied for and duly granted for some of the lads to work on one of the Saturdays.

Saturday morning came around, complete with obligatory hangovers, to find us letting ourselves into the offices. The front doors were locked behind us as we were instructed to do, to prevent any intrusion by undesirables (other than the ones that were working there).

After about one hour or so, with the head still banging in time with the carpenter's hammer, there was an almighty hammering on the front door as though King Kong himself was wishing entry.

Thinking it was one of the lads who was late getting up or someone who had nipped out for a bottle of milk I approached the door with a shout of 'Alright, alright keep your f***ing wig on you impatient b*****d, I'm coming as fast as I f***ing can' – it must have been that marvellous education I had at the University of Life!

Upon opening the door, I sobered up pretty quickly as I looked out into what was patently obviously the barrel of an exceptionally large, official looking, rifle. 'On your knees and put your hands on your head' came an order from the body behind the gun. Imagining I was about to be shot by the IRA, I sank to my knees – involuntarily passing an inordinate amount of wind – as my life flashed before me. This vision of my life was not a pretty sight but nonetheless it was only the added vision of the gun that prevented me from bursting out with laughter about it.

By the way, being an avid fisherman, I had been fishing in Ireland a few times, as did many English lads at that time. This included drinking with the locals in their pubs as well as crossing the border many times at the army checkpoints. None of this had ever been a problem and we had always found the Irish to be very friendly and hospitable.

It was at this point I saw that the front of the building was surrounded by men, some in police uniform, others in plain clothes and almost all of them carrying some sort of firearm – mostly pointed at me. The road was completely blocked by red cars with blue lights on the top as well as police cars of all descriptions. Thinking I was about to be shot by the police instead of the IRA did little to comfort me as a small drop of wee-wee started to dribble down my leg.

Amid much shouting and pointing I was bundled from the building and made to stand on the pavement outside, spread-eagled

45

against the window, as the other guys were quickly rounded up and brought out to a similar fate. After being frisked (hey steady tiger) we were allowed to turn around and put down our hands.

Then came the interrogation. What were we doing in there on a Saturday? How had we gained access? Who was the leader of the gang? What were we after? Where was our helicopter? (Okay I made that bit up!).

After much discussion and subsequent telephone calls it turned out that we had been apprehended by the anti-terrorist squad (better than being picked up by the fuzz though – which can well bring tears to your eyes) as nobody had informed them that we would be working in the building out of office hours, as they were supposed to. 'Another fine mess you've gotten me into Stanley!'

Following about two hours of discussion, and agreements with various bodies, we were allowed back into the building to continue working. Eventually the crowds that had built up dispersed, and normal service was resumed, albeit after three hours of precious time lost (well we had to have a cup of tea following that debacle) and soiled underpants all round.

It certainly gave us something to talk about at tea breaks the following week.

*

This was not the only time that we got on the wrong side of the London police force as it happens.

Working, at another time, in a large, rather prestigious office block in the borough of Chelsea, life was never easy. Our crew were just a small part of a major refurbishment to a large portion of the building, both inside and out. Carrying materials to the eighth floor sometimes occupied a large part of the day, as we were often denied the use of the lift, or the materials were too large to get into the rather ancient cage type lift car. Parking vehicles was also a nightmare, as anyone who has ever attempted to park in central London would appreciate. The parking meters required a constant feeding of pound coins and to park on the double yellow lines outside the building, even to momentarily unload tools and materials, would invite a myriad of wardens to suddenly emerge from the drains and nooks and crannies of London with their pens and pads poised and a vicious leer in their eyes.

Nevertheless, despite all the drawbacks, life, and work, went on relentlessly.

Upon our arrival at the premises one morning, after weeks of the same, we were greeted by a small crowd of onlookers, including two policemen and six burly firefighters peering into the main entrance, from where emerged a cascade of water.

'What is happening?' one of the lads asked innocently.

'There is water flooding throughout the building,' replied one of the bystanders. 'It appears to be coming from the eighth floor, but it is all locked up and no one has a key. We are waiting for the caretaker to come and open it up.'

At the rear of our party of workers someone was heard to mumble 'Oh ****ing hell!' as the plumber slowly collapsed in a crumpled heap onto the pavement.

'Who has the key?' someone in our group asked.

'I have it,' replied another.

'Come on everybody,' shouted the foreman. At that we all surged through the doorway and proceeded to run up the stairs. It was tantamount to trying to scale a waterfall but eventually we reached the eighth floor, and the door was unlocked.

A general moan of 'OH S**T!' went up as the opening of the door released a further torrent of water that had until then been held back. The plumber – whose name has been withheld to save further embarrassment – scrambled over everyone else and half ran, half swam across the floor in order to turn off the stop valve and curb any further flow of water. In fact, the plumber in question still owes me money and I may have to reveal his identity forthwith if remuneration is not forthcoming shortly.

Following the cessation of the surge of water, we all just stood there looking at the plumber as he attempted to crawl up his backside and drag it in after him. Finding out that this was a physical impossibility he was valiantly advised not to cry as there appeared to be enough water around already.

'Has anyone got a sponge'? some wag ventured.

'Anyone want a drink'? someone else cried.

In times of crisis, sympathy was always at a dearth on a building site.

Another voice was heard to cry 'I have a sister who works at the water board if you want a meter'.

After checking his handiwork, the plumber gave forth an explanation. Apparently, the previous afternoon he had fitted a new sink in the kitchen area. This occurrence coincided with the recent innovation of some new type of plumbing fittings. Instead of soldering the fittings to the copper pipe, these were just pushed on and sealed themselves. Brilliant, such a saving in time and bother would surely revolutionise the world! Not for this guy apparently, as I am sure to this day, he has never used any more of them.

He swore at the time that the new fitting had failed and that it was not his fault. It was later proven that he had in fact did not insert the fitting in to its full extent – a very salient point indeed and obviously lack of practise! Millions of these fittings have since been used successfully by people all over the world, and yes, they are an innovation.

Seemingly, it appears that in London, and probably most major cities in England, the water pressure in the public system rises overnight as usage is diminished. This must have caused the joint to fail even though he had tested it at the time, and everything seemed to be alright. This meant that the water had been flowing for a considerable amount of time, at full bore. How many gallons had escaped was anyone's guess, but the damage was obviously immense?

It had flowed through floor after floor, ceiling after ceiling, before the London fire brigade finally pumped out the cellar. Office workers were laid off, computers were thrown into skips, alongside numerous other office objects and the remains of many suspended ceilings and light fittings.

A steady flow of 'suits' entered the building over the next few days, including the premise owners, the landlords, various business owners and many insurance assessors. A major clean up was put into place, and the building resembled a termite mound under attack, as some semblance of order was eventually restored.

Oh, how glad I am that I took up a proper trade instead of becoming a plumber! I know how difficult it can be at times to mess with water – but more of that in another chapter.

It turned out to be an iron fist in a velvet glove for many of us on site. We got so much extra work – paid for, very generously, by the insurance companies, that small fortunes were to be made. The downside of this, for anyone such as me, was that, again, the original contract still had to be finished on time. This meant putting in lots of extra hours at night, often getting back in time just for a quick pint and a kebab before showering and hitting the sack.

One particular night, in the height of the British summer, myself and some of the others were intending to stay until the early hours of the morning, and so as one of the lads went to the take-away for food, I put the kettle on and made the necessary cups of tea. It was a very humid, stuffy night in the middle of London, around twelve midnight. No wind to cool things down (no doubt down to the lack of kebabs) and so we elected to climb out of the window and onto the scaffolding to partake of our refreshments. Not the most picturesque place to have a picnic admittedly but it makes a change from sitting on your toolbox in amongst the debris.

Everything was going fine for about twenty minutes. Then suddenly we were bathed in bright light.

'Funny time for the sun to come out,' someone ventured.

'Do not move, stay right where you are. This is the police, and we are armed' a voice shouted through a megaphone from the pavement.

We had no intention of moving anyway as we had not finished our tea, so we just sat there and awaited developments.

Eventually two faces appeared on the scaffolding below.

'Okay, what is going on here?' asked the one copper.

'We are having a cup of tea. Would you like one?

'Who are you and what are you doing up here at this time of night?

We explained what we were doing and who we were before one of our lads, along with one of the policemen, went down and opened the front door to facilitate letting in the rest of the duly presented half of the Metropolitan police force.

The sergeant in charge eventually informed us that someone in an apartment across the road had reported seeing burglars on the scaffolding obviously breaking into the offices. We explained that burglars do not usually stop to make themselves a cup of tea and that furthermore we would undoubtedly be working late on more than one occasion from now on.

After assuring them that we would not use the *'al fresco'* facilities in future, the boys in blue went merrily on their way, leaving us to carry on working into the wee small hours.

CHAPTER 9

NIGERIA – THE ARMPIT OF THE UNIVERSE

In the late 1970s I became a partner in an electrical contracting company alongside my father and younger brother. Through accident, or fate, we came to export a lot of electrical equipment to a company in Warri in Nigeria. As the managing director of the company in Nigeria was very keen to have a *'White Englishman'* to show off to his business colleagues, and to help procure contracts from companies employing other ex-pats, I found myself aboard an aircraft on my way to Lagos airport on a couple of occasions. Lagos was then the capitol of Nigeria.

Nigeria, at that time was under military rule, and to say that it was lawless and corrupt would be tantamount to saying that the Pope was slightly religious. Coupled with the fact that the only other occasion I had left the United Kingdom was for a honeymoon in Majorca, it was destined to be an experience not to be forgotten in a hurry.

Equipped with some Nigerian money (rather like monopoly money but worth less) and my suitcase I ventured forth, rather like David Livingstone ready to explore the African interior. My naivety, masked by my bravado, would soon begin to show through as the African way of life took its toll on my young, inexperienced body.

At Lagos airport I disembarked the plane to be met with such a blast of heat that at first, I imagined the place was on fire. Surely nowhere could be this hot and sticky naturally. I blinked my eyes, and this action was enough to start a torrent of sweat streaming from every pore in my body as I followed the throng across the tarmac toward the 'terminal'. Whoever decided that terminology for an airport building had obviously had Lagos in mind as this place was most definitely on its last legs. I survived the trek across the airport only by being extremely vigilant. It seemed that anyone on foot was fair game for a mowing down by anyone driving a vehicle of any shape or size and it quickly became obvious that Nigeria was not an orderly, organised, safe environment akin to the England I had left far behind.

Upon retrieving my suitcase from the carousel, I made my way through the sick, sorry, terminal building, pushed, bumped, and crowded at every step only to arrive at immigration control. Handing over my 'British' passport I confidently stood waiting for a smile and a 'Thank-you Sir, you may proceed.' Instead, I was faced with an extremely black, surly, fun hating guy, built like a brick outhouse, and dressed in a uniform that was three sizes too small and was probably really smart the day it was first worn – about thirty years ago judging from the condition of it. No self-respecting moth would ever have flown within yards of it never mind have subjected its young to such a meal by laying its eggs anywhere in the general vicinity.

'Is this your first visit to Nigeria?' Bellowed 'Happy Jack.'

'Yes,' I timidly replied, suitably intimidated, my legs turning to jelly.

'Wait here,' he grunted as he wandered off with my passport, as if I were thinking of making a break for it into the African interior without my most treasured possession.

After about ten minutes of profuse perspiring and feeling the urgent need to use the toilet, I had convinced myself that my fate was to spend the rest of my miserable existence in a cockroach infested fleapit, sitting on a concrete bench, behind steel bars, eating rats that I had caught and being repeatedly raped by large black inmates. Okay I had probably watched too much television, but as time went on my imagination lent itself to all manner of terrible outcomes. A good job I was innocent really, I do not know what I would have conjured up if I had been carrying a quantity of some illicit drug.

Eventually he returned with the slightest hint of a smile on his ugly face. This turned into a full-blown grin, showing a set of teeth like a row of tombstones, as he rejoiced in telling me that there was a problem with my visa.

'But I went to the Nigerian embassy to get it,' I squeaked.

'I do not care if you got it out of a Christmas cracker,' boomed my new-found friend. 'It is a problem for you. Fortunately, I have had a word with my supervisor, and he can rectify the problem for you, but it will cost you some money.'

The little light bulb in my head illuminated as I realised what was going on. I had been warned that getting anything or anywhere could be subject to 'DASH'. This was the bribery that was so profuse at the time and short of sitting around for hours and missing my connecting flight, or turning around and returning to England, I had no choice but to pay the going rate. Unfortunately for me, as this was my first experience of such a way of life, I had no idea what the 'going rate' was, so foolishly enquired as to how much was required of me. I was *'lucky?'* that I had managed to procure some local currency before embarking on my 'Doctor Livingstone' adventure.

The gears could be heard turning inside his head as he imagined all his birthdays rolled into one had just presented themselves on a plate. Faced with such a dilemma it took a while to conjure up an appropriate amount. 'Five hundred naira' exploded from his grin, which was by this time almost splitting his face in half.

Before I had collected my thoughts, I said, 'That is a ridiculous amount of money.' As soon as the words had left my mouth, I could taste that rat again and feel my trousers being forcibly removed.

As the grin left his face, I felt my bowels begin to loosen before he said menacingly, 'Okay I will get him to accept two hundred.'

Suddenly my confidence rose as I realised the way that this 'game' was obviously meant to be played. I put my hand in my pocket and pulled out a one hundred naira note. Passing it through the hatch, I defiantly looked him squarely in the eyes, at the same time slipping another one hundred naira note off the wad in my pocket, just in case.

Without another word he stamped my passport and handed it back, whilst deftly slipping the note into his pocket. I grabbed my passport and proceeded on my way; one hundred naira poorer but richer in the knowledge that I supposedly knew how to survive the weeks ahead. My confidence boosted, I looked around for the Nigerian Airways desk to check in for my flight to Benin, ready to begin another round of negotiation in order to board this flight. Fortunately, this leg of the journey passed without incidence, and I boarded the flight empowered by my experience.

*

Upon my arrival in Benin, as per my instructions, I went to find a taxi to take me to my final destination in Warri. Being the only white man for miles around, I stood out like a blind cobbler's thumb and was soon enveloped by taxi drivers, 'porters', beggars, lepers, and other undesirables, all willing to relieve me of my cash by fair means or foul.

Grabbing on to the largest inhabitant – about six feet four in bare feet and built like the Berlin wall – for protection I said, 'I need a taxi to Warri'. Immediately sensing a profit, he started shouting furiously in some language unknown to me. The crowd reluctantly dispersed with amazing alacrity, except the lepers and other beggars with no legs who slowly shuffled away. 'I have the best taxi in Benin for you,' replied my latest newfound best friend. Leading me across the pothole ridden dirt road, grasping my suitcase as if it were a small lunch box, he led me to a line of cars.

In my wisdom I thought we were passing a scrap yard, but it turned out this was actually the taxi rank! Loading my case into an excuse for a car he proceeded to tie the boot shut with a piece of string. I looked at the car convinced that he was having a laugh at my expense. The tyres were bald as a baby's arse, the bumper (singular) was hanging off and again tied up with string, the doors were barely able to close, the make totally unidentifiable and the fact that it had more dents than a beaten copper dish, did nothing to convince me that this vehicle (sic) could even make it to the gates of the airport, never mind my destination. How was I to get out of this alive? Discretion being the better part of valour, I decided that to die in a car accident was probably less painful than arguing with the man mountain before me, who would undoubtedly delight in chewing me up and spitting out the bones – yes, I was convinced that cannibalism was still rife in some if not all parts of Africa.

Hiding in the rear seat, or what remained of it – it looked as if someone had been to a drive-in movie, not enjoyed the film, and slashed the seats – as we hurtled down dirt roads at break-neck speed I was relieved when we halted at a petrol pump sat by the side of the road. I swear that the driver stopped by hurling an anchor from the window as compensation for the inadequate (if indeed existent) braking system.

'I need money for petrol' growled the grizzly bear in the front seat. Wishing at this stage that I could disappear down one of the holes in the excuse for a seat, I whined 'how much do you need?'

'One hundred naira will be enough for now.' Handing over the appropriate note, I settled down for the rest of the sort of ride that people pay good money to endure at Blackpool. Apart from stopping briefly at the military checkpoints, the rest of the journey seemed pretty uneventful – at least to me curled up on the back seat, eyes tightly closed it did. At one point the driver did enquire, after swerving around a bend in the road, 'Can you smell something funny?' to which my reply was, 'Smell it, I'm sitting in it!'

We arrived at my destination – the offices of an electrical contracting company – at which point the driver politely asked for another four hundred naira. Alighting from the car, I was suddenly surrounded by a sea of black faces, looking at me as if I had just landed from another planet. The crowd parted as the boss appeared, introduced himself and led me into his premises. 'I need to pay the taxi man his fare,' I said as I was shown to a seat.

'How much is it? I will take care of it,' replied my new carer.

'Four hundred Naira, as I have already paid him one hundred to fill up of petrol.' The blood momentarily drained from his face before it refilled to overflowing. Never before had I seen a black face go a whiter shade of pale followed by crimson. He obviously disagreed with the potential extortion. Bellowing some obviously profound words in his own language, he stormed outside and started shouting at the taxi driver. Clearly unable to understand the conversations taking place, I could only stand and watch as an angry exchange of words took place, closely followed by further men appearing from the adjoining workshop wielding machetes and various sized pieces of wood. The last I saw of the taxi, it was hurtling up the road, boot open, being pursued by an angry mob, and pelted with stones. As I was soon to find out, justice is swift, brutal – and very often fatal in Nigeria.

*

I was given a room, in a motel, where all my expenses were paid by the company that I was representing. I think this is where my everlasting liking for brandy really took off, as the beer was the usual insipid lager that seems to be produced all over the world. The bar in the motel was frequented by many ex-pats, from all corners of the world, and I became friends with quite a few before long, especially as when it came to my round. I just signed the docket, and everyone had a good time. I got to know a lot of the local news quite quickly from these friends.

I soon found out about a taxi that had refused to stop at one of the military roadblocks. The driver, along with the two white girl passengers in the rear seat, were shot to bits before going very far up the road. As I said, retribution in Nigeria came quickly and deadly.

I had not been there awfully long when one night there was a commotion on the road outside the motel. It was difficult to differentiate the noise from the usual nightly barrage but there definitely seemed to be something going down, as signified by all the shouting and screaming going on. Most nights were filled with the sound of music – no not the film – of various reggae and black artists, especially Barry White, who at that time was a particular favourite. To this day I hate all reggae, and similar music after lying awake night after night listening to it thumping through the walls and windows of my motel room, even drowning out the whistling and clanking of the unmaintained air conditioning unit. Upon waking the next morning, I went to breakfast and enquired as to what had happened in the early hours of the morning. I was informed that an armed robber had been captured the previous day and put in the local jail. Someone decided that he was obviously guilty, without the bother of a trial – a mere formality apparently. He was forcibly removed from the jail by a mob, taken to the nearest suitable tree, and had his neck stretched there and then by a rope and a cheering crowd of onlookers.

I must admit, I always ensured that from that night on I behaved impeccably and used all the locks on my bedroom door every night.

*

After a couple of weeks had passed, I was asked to accompany the managing director of the company to a football match in Benin and although not a lover of soccer – I prefer to watch a man's game, rugby – it was important for him to be seen with an English man in his company and so I agreed.

This would be the first time I had been on a long car journey since my taxi ride, but I knew that the Volvo we would be going in was infinitely more comfortable and looked forward to getting away from the confines of the proximity of Warri if only for a short while.

It was certainly an eventful day out as it turned out.

Before too long we were at the first roadblock. The chauffeur opened the window and exchanged dialogue with the two soldiers – two scary looking, heavily armed soldiers, I may add. After about a minute he threw something out of the driver's window. At this point, the soldiers fell scrabbling to the floor whilst the chauffeur put his foot to the boards and took off at a mighty pace. Remembering the tale of the taxi being shot up, I dived into the foot well. Fortunately, I had by this time taken to carrying a spare pair of underpants everywhere with me as the Nigerian food did not always agree with me and accidents were sometimes inevitable. This time it was not so much an accident, as an involuntary reaction to the situation. The managing director sat looking at me, thinking that this was perhaps some strange English Pagan ritual, before enquiring why I was curled up in a ball, quivering like a jelly and smelling rather peculiar.

Eventually, I arose and explained my actions and enquired as to what the driver had thrown and why we were still alive. He explained that the driver always kept a bucket of coins by his seat and at each roadblock would throw a handful of coins for the soldiers, who were far more interested in retrieving them than worrying about us. It did not do much for my confidence to live to see another day, but it turned out it was effective in every case. Money is everything in a place like that.

Further up the road, we came up behind an articulated truck that was swerving all over the road quite violently, forcing vehicles coming the other way to drive into the storm drains that lined the roadsides. I was reliably informed that the driver of the truck was obviously drunk on kai-kai (the native gin distilled from the sap of the palm trees) or as high as a kite on marijuana. Either way it looked as if our day out was quickly coming to an end. I expected my friend to instruct the driver to turn around, but no, this is Nigeria and a small problem like this would not prevent us from reaching our destination. Fortunately, not being able to speak Igbo left me ignorant of the instruction to the driver. Taking his opportunity, the driver changed down the gears, floored the accelerator, and sped past the truck as he swerved to the nearside. Not being a religious person, I did not have a rosary to cling to but certainly prayed to someone or something at that moment, whilst at the same time making a mental note to buy more pairs of underpants to carry on my person in future!

We survived the journey to Benin and joined the vast crowd making their way toward the football stadium. Football always was a big thing in Nigeria and attracted masses of people, some not intent on cheering on the winning side. Doing an impression of a sardine in a tin, I was carried along by the throng, a lone white face in a sea of black – I looked like a one/blank domino. The English were much respected on the whole and I have to say that much reverence was given to me all through my ordeal of being in the country – especially when it came to be relieving me of my money. As I was carried along by the sweaty, smelly, but generally well-behaved crowd I felt a hand deftly making its way too close to my nether regions. Being a red-blooded male, definitely of a heterosexual nature, I plunged my hand down to find out what was going on, only to find another hand making its way into my pocket. Grabbing a hold of the said hand, I raised it up and twisted it at the same time. Next to me a scrawny youth with a face like a chewed wine gum began yelling in pain. My friend enquired as to the problem, and I informed him that I had caught this chap with his hand in my pocket. He immediately started shouting in Igbo at him and the last I saw, as I was whisked away, was this spotty pickpocket disappearing to the ground, in a cloud of dust and flailing arms and legs, whilst being beaten and kicked by a frenzied crowd. I was told that he would receive his punishment for his attempted crime and indeed would be lucky to escape with his life.

The day that stared out so ordinary became a day that is forever etched on my mind.

*

Whilst in Nigeria I caught malaria, despite taking the extremely expensive quinine tablets obtained from my doctor at home. Fortunately, it was not one of the more virulent strains, thankfully – my father ended up in the tropical diseases department of a Birmingham hospital with his. Even so, it is far from pleasant and recurred intermittently for many years after.

I also suffered a few times from the usual stomach upsets that beleaguers most intrepid explorers – Doctor Livingstone eat your heart out! On one occasion that comes to mind, after lying awake all night, sweating and moaning and rolling around the bed, in between frequent, relatively fast, dashes to the toilet, I was roused by the driver who had come to collect me. Collating all my strength, I fell out of bed and crawled to the door. Opening it, I explained the problem to the driver who went and telephoned the boss of the company and then came back to collect me.

As I writhed around on the rear seat, I was duly driven to a clinic on the outskirts of town, only too aware that I was probably going to have my life firmly placed in the hands of the local witch doctor. I was too ill by this time, to worry, sure that my last lifeblood was fast draining away. Fortunately, the driver was equipped with the necessary 'dash' to facilitate prompt attention, much to the annoyance of the irate crowds who had probably been queuing for a matter of days. Instead of a monkey's hand and a collection of herbs stewed together, as I was expecting, I was soon treated to a pain killing injection. When I say pain killing, I mean it killed the pain in my stomach. Administered firmly into my left buttock, the ensuing pain – which had the effect of making me crawl up the wall – screaming and hanging from the light fitting – was enough to ensure that I never went back there again. It seemed to fix the stomach cramps and associated 'runs' but also ensured that I could not sit comfortably on that cheek for a good six weeks after. It is probably just as well that I could not understand the local dialect as I am sure the conversation that ensued was something about the young white Nancy boy that could not even stand a little prick (well I have never been that way inclined anyway).

After being delivered back to my motel room, armed with plenty of bottled water, I retired to the refuge of my bed, after ensuring that the 'Do not disturb' sign was hung on the doorknob.

As I was lying in my bed, feeling sorry for myself and wishing I were at home, a little voice spoke to me.

"Smile, things could be worse!"

Knowing deep in my heart that this was undoubtedly true, I beamed a big smile to myself.

The voice of wisdom obviously spoke the truth as, lo and behold, things did get worse!

Sometime, during the following fitful sleep, I dreamed that someone was hammering on my door. Weakly whispering 'go away' to the dream, I settled down to continue my much-needed sleep. Some dreams just refuse to leave though, and this was one of them. The persistent hammering on the door came out of the dream and became a reality. There really was someone intent on disturbing my much-needed slumber.

Again, falling out of bed and dragging myself hand over hand over to the door, I sat there and opened it slowly. Standing there was a member of the motel staff holding my 'Do not disturb' sign.

'Sorry, Massa,' he beamed. 'Just needed to tell you your sign had fallen off the door.'

Unable to physically rip his head off his shoulders at that moment in time, all I could think to say was 'Thanks'.

He duly replaced the sign and as I crawled back to bed, I could hear him whistling to himself as he made his rounds, happy to have done his good deed for the day. I am sure Mr Baden-Powell would have been proud to know that his rules were being obeyed, even in the bowels of the jungle.

*

After a few weeks it was time to leave, and I was chauffeured to Benin airport for my return to Lagos. Sitting in the departure lounge I spotted another white face and went across to sit and talk to someone who probably spoke the mother tongue (as opposed to the mother-in-law's tongue, but that is another story). Unfortunately, he hailed from Glasgow, so conversation was stilted to say the least. Still, at least he did speak a version of English that was slightly more understandable than the Nigerian version. Time crept on and my Glaswegian friend said in his best accent, 'Ye'd better grab yer briefcase. They'll be calling oor flight soon.'

'That's alright I have a confirmed ticket,' I replied, fishing my ticket from my pocket.

Staring at me as if I were stupid (which could carry just a hint of truth) he said, 'You've no done this before have ye.'

'Nay,' I replied in my best Glaswegian accent, 'incidentally, I have since survived a walk doon Sauchiehall Street in the centre of Glasgow, at 11 o'clock at night – not a mean feat at the time.'

'Well, I can tell yoo now that just because you have an OK ticket, doesnae mean ye'll get on the 'plane'.'

'What do you mean?'

'There'll be more tickets than seats, I can guarantee you that.'

'They can't do that.'

'They can and they will. When I run, run after me.'

Not being the sort of man that runs after other men I hesitated, but not for long as an announcement started, and 'Jock' fled. Grabbing my briefcase, I swiftly followed across the tarmac, like Usain Bolt with a lion hot on his heels, to the waiting Nigerian Airways rust bucket. By now I was starting to panic and elbowed my way up the steps as seemed to be the 'norm'. Diving into one of the few vacant seats left, a familiar voice came from behind, 'See what I mean Jimmy.'

A few rows erupted amongst the passengers unable to procure a seat but eventually the doors were closed, and a collective sigh of relief was heard. It was at this point that I suddenly realised that my suit jacket was still on the back of the seat in the departure lounge. I knew there was no chance of retrieving it, but it was a small price to pay for a lesson well learned.

*

On the second occasion that I went to Nigeria I was a lot wiser to the protocol regarding money changing hands and therefore was a lot better prepared.

Upon arrival I lined up with everyone else at the carousel to retrieve my luggage. I have since found out that no matter how early or late you check in, Murphy's Law dictates that your suitcase is always amongst the last few to arrive on the conveyor belt. Patiently waiting until there was only the obligatory one unclaimed case left, it dawned on me that my luggage had done a disappearing act.

Making my way to the Lufthansa desk, I duly queued up, British style.

Anyone who has ever been to such a third world country will probably know that the British are the only ones who queue. In

Nigeria everyone pushes to the front of the crowd thrusting forward a hand, usually clutching the necessary documentation and remuneration, and sounding off a constant stream of 'SSSS', 'SSSS', 'SSSS', "SSSS'. The first time it happened I was not sure if someone had released a crate full of snakes or the luggage trolley was suffering a series of fast punctures. But no, it turned out that this is the only way to attract the attention of whoever is on the desk.

Eventually my patient queuing paid off – probably because I was the only person still standing at the desk – and a rather indifferent voice enquired as to the nature of my problem. Upon explaining that my suitcase had gone to the place where all the odd socks go, I was given a form to fill in and told that my suitcase would be delivered to my motel the following day – guaranteed. No problem then, I could survive twenty-four hours without surely – do not call me Shirley ever again! Well, perhaps on alternate Fridays. My gratitude upon hearing this was met with a smile, no doubt something to do with the twenty naira note that was being stuffed into his greasy little mitt. Yes, I knew how to ensure things got done.

Because my flight got in quite late, I had a room booked for the night at the airport hotel. After checking in and going to my room I realised that not only could I not have a shave and apply some deodorant but that the only shirt I had, that was on my back, was by now dripping with sweat. I had no choice but to wash my shirt in the basin and put it on the balcony to dry whilst having a thorough wash, before going down to dinner. I had to hope that the creases would be viewed as a new British fashion statement. It was whilst hanging out the shirt that I heard a tremendous roaring sound and looked up to see an extremely large passenger airplane heading directly for me. Diving for cover behind the wardrobe – as if that would be sufficient to cushion the impact – I realised that in fact the hotel was at the end of the runway and that said plane was merely taking off, albeit within inches of my room. Even the offer of a bribe failed to secure a replacement room as the hotel was full. Needless to say, despite the sedative qualities of a 'few' Remy Martin cognacs, little sleep was had in between the various landings and take-offs that seemed to last all night.

The following day, I was met at Benin airport by the Volvo and driver who enquired as to where my suitcase was. I explained that it had gone astray and was to be delivered to my motel later that day – naivety can sometimes be a blessing.

Two days later, it was blatantly obvious my suitcase was still nowhere to be seen. The managing director took me out and bought me new clothes, shaving kit and above all deodorant as I must have looked like a tramp and smelt like Grimsby docks on a hot day. Not the sort of impression he wanted me to portray to his prospective clients. Happy days! Despite constant telephone calls, my suitcase never appeared during the following five weeks, and I was incredibly grateful for the new clothes that were constantly procured in order for me to look respectable to meet new clients.

Upon my return to Lagos airport, I stormed over to the Lufthansa desk, ready for a row, but as usual apathy roles OK! Upon stating my case (actually, my case was still missing) I was directed to an airplane hangar across the other side of the airport. This apparently was the missing luggage store, reached by precariously skirting the runway and avoiding any jumbo jets landing or taking off. I entered the hangar only to be confronted with about ten million suitcases, amongst various other detritus – although no odd socks were espied – all lined up on racking as well as on the floor. Alright perhaps that is a slight exaggeration, but there was a lot. Just inside the hangar, sat in a ramshackle, makeshift office, constructed from packing cases that had obviously never been re-united with their rightful owners, sat a little Nigerian airport official, smiling and showing a set of extremely white and large teeth. They were probably part of the lost property originally, but now sat in a mouth that wore a permanent smile due to the fact that they were too large for the mouth that held them. Given the poor light conditions it was fortunate that they were so bright and enabled me to see that he was actually in there.

I have come to find my case, I hope,' I said, envisaging a weeklong treasure hunt amongst the rows of dust covered bounty.

'Yes, Massa; he slobbered through his – originally someone else's – gnashers. What is the name?'

'Mr Jones – Alan Jones.'

As he picked his jaw up off the floor (I am not sure if this was due to shock or the weight of the dentures) he tried a sickly smile as if to say that it was in here somewhere.

'How long ago did you lose it?'

'I did not lose it, Lufthansa mislaid it.'

'Ah! Lufthansa. So, it will be in this row,' he confidently stated, pointing to the left-hand side. 'I remember now, I have been looking after it special for you.'

'Well, that narrows it down to about ten thousand,' I sarcastically replied. 'Well at least as you have been looking after it for me, you will know exactly where it is will you not?'

Looking very sheepish – it could have something to do with the teeth – he hesitantly said, 'I forgot now exactly where I put it.'

Amazing that, so hard to believe! I knew it was going to be down to me to find it and after slowly sifting through the many suitcases, of various colours and sizes, I eventually spied one the right size and colour.

'This looks like it,' I said hopefully, as I reached up and lifted down my long-lost treasure.

Heaving it on to the floor, I looked at *'toothy'* and said, 'So you have looked after it especially for me huh?'

'Yes, Massa, I remember which one it was now.'

'So why is it like this then?' I asked, whilst turning the case around to reveal the damage, where the hinge had obviously been deliberately released from the body of the case. I unlocked the case and looked inside. It was blatantly obvious that a hand had rifled through the contents, and I could immediately see that my electric razor was missing.

'It must have been the man that is here at night. I always thought he looked a little shifty,' he coyly replied. A rich statement coming from him, I thought, only at this point noticing how nice and clean shaven he was.

I did and said no more but lifted my case and made to leave the building before I had a tantrum and started stamping my feet – preferably on his head. My friend decided that this was his cue to stand in the doorway and pulling himself up to his full five feet four inches stated, 'Do not forget that I looked after it for you.'

Fast losing control, unable to believe that he had the sheer brass neck to expect a *'tip'* I exploded.

'You expect f*****g dash for f*****g looking after my f*****g case, you thieving little b*****d. I ought to rip your f*****g head off your f*****g shoulders. You have more chance of f*****g knitting fog than getting f*****g money from me, you little s**t'

Realising that I was in a foreign country and hoping to catch my flight home I realised that I had to be the bigger man. Well, that was easy, so I strode past him and made my way back to the airport terminal followed by mouthfuls of abuse in various languages beyond my comprehension. As the vicious tirade came to a rather abrupt end, I turned to see him fawning and slobbering around his next victim like a spider inviting a fly into his web.

I thought about reporting him but decided it would probably entail more dash and endless form filling, so I decided to put it down to experience and an insurance claim.

*

Upon my return to the terminal, I made my way to the check in desk, happy to be returning to some sort of sanity at last – I am easy pleased after all as you have no doubt worked out. Confidently flashing my ticket across the desk, I awaited my boarding card, glad that I was still in time for my flight even though it was starting to get a little close due to the fiasco with my suitcase.

'Mr. Jones,' a little voice squeaked from below the desk.

'That's me,' I replied, confidently handing over my passport for confirmation.

'Sorry to tell you but your name is not on the manifest,' said the little maggot behind the desk.

'No, you must be mistaken, that is an OK ticket, and it was confirmed by telephone a few days ago,' I re-iterated.

'I can assure you that your name is not on the manifest Mr. Jones. And what is more I cannot see it on the stand-by list.'

Suddenly I remembered what the game was and dipped my hand into my pocket. Passing over the obligatory twenty naira note, I stated 'I think you will find my name is on the manifest.'

'No, sorry your name is not on my manifest, but I will look again on the stand-by.'

My hand flew across the desk speedily issuing a further monetary inducement.

'Yes, you are right,' he replied, pocketing the note faster than the speed of light. 'Your name is on the stand-by list, but it is a long way down.'

'I think you will find that it is in fact at the top of the list,' I retorted whilst greasing his grubby little paw with another, higher denomination note.

'You are so right; I must have missed it there.'

It was at this point that the flight was called, and people began slowly making their way towards the departure lounge. I determined not to move far from the desk so that I could avail of my position at the top of the 'stand-by list' as soon as possible. Time went by and despite my numerous enquiries, no information as to my chances of catching the flight were forthcoming.

Eventually, with only about twenty minutes to take off I was handed a boarding card and proceeded to make my way in the general direction of the awaiting airplane. As this was my second departure from Lagos, I was only too aware of the fact that I had still to go through Immigration Control, Health Control, Passport Control, Currency Control and Customs as well as any other desk that could be imagined and put into commission as another way of parting me with my hard-earned cash. Strictly speaking it was money that I had been given by the company in Nigeria for expenses, but I am not one to split hairs – although I would have made an exception for 'Goofy' in the lost property department – with a machete! Although you were not allowed to take the Nigerian currency out of the country, it was the only way to ensure a safe passage to the awaiting airplane. Quite why you were not allowed to remove their currency was not clear, as if you did bring some back to England even the main banks would not exchange it for you, but that is the way the law was at that time.

Most of the people behind the desks were quite covert in their requests for bribery but one 'gentleman' – and I use the word very loosely – at the customs desk, actually said, 'Do you want to catch that plane'?

'Of course I do,' I said, already digging into my pocket for the money.

'Then you give me money,' he replied.

It actually cost, on this occasion, all the Naira that I had left, plus twenty pounds sterling in order to get to climb the stairs to the airplane – just as they were about to be removed. Never have I been so relieved to be parted with my cash.

*

That was the last I ever saw of Nigeria, as the toerag that was the owner of the business, we were supplying materials to, managed to rip us off to the tune of many tens of thousands of pounds.

Although I was destined never to set foot there again, I often wondered how he got on with the enormous diesel generating set that we sent out to him. It was for the large contract at the University of Benin and cost hundreds of thousands of pounds, being a very large machine complete with a Rolls Royce engine. Unfortunately, due to a mistake at the shipper's, the custom-built control panel failed to be shipped with it. I know for a fact that it was never sent, and I wonder, even to this day, how, or if, it was ever started up.

I must admit, that being a good Christian soul, I prayed for him every night for many months. Whether my prayers were ever answered, and he died a long, slow extremely painful death, I do not know. I think I still have the doll I made but after sticking pins in it so frequently it began to deteriorate.

Having your own business – all play and no work – happy days, eh?

CHAPTER 10

SECRETS AND TRUE LIES

Sometimes, circumstances came about where I was left alone in a strange house and secrets were unearthed accidentally. Sometimes secrets were revealed by the owners of the property voluntarily.

One of the former occasions came about whilst I was working for a company that became quite famous by appearing on television – for all the wrong reasons.

Unfortunately for them, the programme was a consumer protection programme, and they were ripped limb from limb – quite rightly so as the management were a right bunch of cowboys as I found out to my cost. But, as the saying goes, there is no such thing as bad publicity and the company just closed down, only to re-open the following day under another name.

I can remember going for the interview, at their office in Leamington Spa. I was told that some of their guys were earning three hundred pounds per week, which at that time was huge money. As a married man with a mortgage and about to start a family, this was what I needed and could not wait to get started. Unfortunately, they conveniently forgot to mention the fact that you were self-employed. Also, there was a little matter of actually getting the money that you had earned – most of it by awfully long hours and extremely hard graft.

The work entailed fitting electric showers – easy enough for an electrician – although you had to do the plumbing and the tiling as ell. Oh, and anything else such as carpentry and installing a shower base and enclosure that enabled you to fit the shower in the first place. And drilling through two-foot-thick Welsh solid stone walls. The sales team pressured people into signing up for a shower even where it was virtually impossible to fit them. Once they had their papers signed and had their commissions paid, it was left up to the installers to explain why it was not possible for them to have a shower.

After travelling many miles to do the job – in the brand-new van supplied (by the way we also forgot the fact that you have to supply the petrol) – it was sometimes exceedingly difficult to explain to an irate customer that it just is not possible to fit a shower into an area where there is no water supply and no chance of drainage for the shower base that was also required. The rub was that if you did not do the job, you did not get any money for it either.

The other aspect was that the sales reps always took a deposit and then – providing that the job was at all possible – it was then up to the installer, on completion, to collect the balance due. This sometimes was paid in cash, but more often was in the form of a finance agreement – pushed by the sales as a way of getting more commission. It was necessary to get the satisfaction note signed and delivered back to the office in order for the finance agreement to kick in. Most customers wanted to wait a week before sending in the signed note just to make sure that everything was satisfactory, as agreed at the time of the sale. Failure to return the signed note – or the cash balance – meant that the installer only received half of the money due; until such time that the note was received. As time went on, the list of half paid jobs became longer and longer, despite weekly enquiries and complaints to the office – another obviously contrived way of cheating the installer, but one that had you tied in almost watertight. It was almost impossible to leave the job, as you were owed so much money, money that would never be forthcoming if you left. As time wore on, the prospects that seemed so good at the interview became a more distant memory.

*

Monday mornings became a nightmare as you never knew what the week ahead held in store. I well remember one Monday in particular. I had returned on the preceding Saturday from a week's camping holiday – all that we could afford in those days.

I walked into the office to receive my work. Your week's work was always handed out to you on Monday morning, all arranged chronologically and organised with the customers. The theory of that was fine, but it meant that you had to finish the job, or jobs, allocated for each day in order to reach the next day's work on schedule. Sometimes this would entail two *'simple'* jobs in a day, although they could be miles apart from each other and to work late into the night was far from unusual, in order to fit it all in. The other side of the coin was that if you arrived to find that it was not possible to do the installation, you had no work to carry on with and a day's money would be gone. Oh, the joys of the self-employed! On this particular occasion, I walked in and was handed the work sheets for the week. South Wales – every job!

Being a nice, polite fellow, I said, 'Excuse me, I am deeply sorry, but I cannot do South Wales this week as I have just come back from holiday and have no money for petrol, lodgings, food etc, apart from the fact that most of my clothes are waiting to be washed.'

'Oh, sorry about that. In that case we do not have any work for you this week then,' came the candid reply. Sympathy was not on the menu from the office staff, especially on a Monday morning. Or Tuesday, Wednesday, Thursday, and Friday.

Not working for a week was not an option at this point in my life, so reluctantly I left the office, not knowing how I was even going to get to Wales, never mind eat, sleep, and fill the petrol tank for a week. I went home and packed a spare pair of socks, underpants etc. into a bag and then, leaving a note of explanation for my wife, who was at work (no mobile phones), went cap in hand to my parent's house. They were surprised to see me on the doorstep doffing my cap as I never usually wore one. Fortunately, they lent me some money for petrol and crisps and off I went for the week, sulking but able to survive.

I believe this was the beginning of getting used to sleeping in the confines of a van. It certainly was not the last time it happened. I became very adept at curling up on the front seat of a van or car, or quite often on the floor of an office or shop if the opportunity arose. My trusty sleeping bag and blankets travelled many miles with me throughout my working life and were called to action whenever finances dictated or for grabbing a couple of hours whilst working a 'ghoster'.

*

So, off I went to deepest South Wales. Up the valleys, boyo – where the men are men, and the sheep are terrified (sorry Richard).

The first job (Monday's) on the list required me to pick up the key from the neighbour's house which I duly did. This was not an unusual situation as a lot of people were reluctant to take a day off work just to oversee a job that according to the salesperson 'will only take a couple of hours'. If only they had been made to actually go out and fit some – or at least see the work that was involved. But a sale was a sale to them and damn the consequences and the fitter.

Upon picking up the key I was informed by the neighbour that she was surprised at being asked to hold it, as the couple that lived there were very private and kept themselves to themselves most of the time as far as the neighbours were concerned. 'Mind you, there is a lot of comings and goings. They appear to have a lot of friends who come around occasionally and stay rather late,' she informed me.

Don't you just love nosey neighbours who make it their business to know everyone else's?

At least I knew that the client would know, and hopefully appreciate, when they retrieved the key, that the job *'did not only take a couple of hours'*. Indeed, I would probably still be toiling away when they arrived home from work, as by the time I had reached my destination the day was wearing away rapidly.

I turned the key in the door, slowly opened the door and shouted loudly, 'Hello, anyone in?' This was brought about by the aftermath of a previous job where the house was supposed to be empty. After I had worked away for about an hour, a pimply, long-haired youth stepped wearily and butt naked from a bedroom, only to almost disappear down the lifted floorboards on the landing. I do not know who had the biggest shock. I only know that as I was kneeling down on the landing, feeding in a cable, I was at the right (or wrong) height to look up and see a naked persons nether region getting precariously close to collapsing on top of me. I am sure he was not pleased to see me as he had no idea I was there and can only presume that he was suffering from the complaint that many young men suffer from early in the morning prior to a visit to the bathroom. He shot back into his bedroom, whilst I sat there wondering why I could not have taken his turn in the queue when they were handing out the 'fire-fighting equipment'.

It transpired that his parents had not informed him of my possible presence as he would be at work, but he had woken up with a sore throat, turned over and entered the comatose state beloved of the youth. Upon waking, he had dreamily gone to go to the bathroom. We apologised, and explained to one another, and he sheepishly disappeared back to his 'stinking pit', after the much-needed visit to the bathroom, thankfully wearing his underpants this time.

Anyway, back to the house in Wales. No one answered and I made my way into the hallway ready to commence battle with whatever lay ahead.

Now I have always been an avid reader of books, and at that

particular time was heavily into Dennis Wheatley amongst other weird stuff. For those who are not aware of whom Dennis Wheatley was, he was a very prolific writer from the 1930s through to the 1960s. He was a very descriptive writer, and a lot of his novels involved the occult. Black magic to me, at that time, definitely did not involve a box of chocolates.

I could not help noticing, upon entering the house, the profusion of black candles placed strategically around.

Putting this down to a whim I continued through the house. A general look around the premises was always the first thing on the agenda. This was firstly to ascertain that no knife wielding maniac was lurking unexpectedly, and secondly to gain a knowledge of the layout of the premises and the position of the electrical equipment. It soon came to my attention that the presence of the black candles in the hallway was not the only evidence of dark forces at work in the house. Tarot cards, more black candles, books on unusual subjects, packets of salt, a lock of hair and a pentagram chalked on the floor quickly confirmed that the 'Neighbourhood Watch' was not aware that she was living next door to the 'Neighbourhood Witch.'

I was not unduly concerned, after all people are entitled to their own little idiosyncrasies, especially in their own homes. Nevertheless, the job was carried out in near record time in order that I had vacated the premises before the occupants returned from work. I left a message for them to send in the satisfaction note. Another job I only received half the money for, but this time I felt it was justified as being much safer than returning later under the cover of darkness.

*

Another incident that comes to mind, whilst working for the same motley crew, was at a house in Birmingham, this time much closer to home. As I stated earlier, I was expected to carry out the plumbing etc, which was normally straightforward enough. A pipe joined into the mains cold feed at an appropriate point and fed straight into the shower was easy-peasy for an electrician who was faced constantly with far more difficult conundrums.

This certain house was a large Victorian establishment in a rather posh part of Birmingham – yes, there are still posh parts of 'Brum' – if you know where to look.

It seemed that truly little modernisation work had been applied for many years and upon inspection found that the electrical side of the installation would be easy enough. The plumbing however was a different matter, as upon inspecting the pipe work it was all found to be lead pipes in the bathroom and very awkward to access. I investigated the loft and found that although there was still only lead piping, it was far easier to get to and so decided that was where my main line of plumbing attack would be.

Being the sort of company that ran to tight margins, regarding materials and wages, (indeed it was rumoured that the boss was so tight that when he walked, his arse squeaked, although this was unconfirmed as I had never seen the fat slob leave his chair) we were issued only with stainless steel pipe instead of copper to carry out the job. Anyone who has ever attempted to cut stainless steel with a hacksaw will know that it is like trying to beat someone's brains out with a piece of wet string, but copper pipe was far too expensive for 'Lard-Arse.'

Even with my limited knowledge of plumbing I knew that you could not join stainless steel onto lead and therefore a trip to the local plumber's merchant was called for. More of my petrol to be wasted, along with the cost of the extra materials, which would no doubt not be reimbursed for one reason or another. Still, I had another job scheduled for the afternoon and so time was at a premium.

I informed the owners of the house where I was going and why.

'You will be finished, today, won't you?' asked the man of the house.

'Yes, of course, I have another job to do this afternoon,' I replied.

'Only we are going away on holiday early in the morning and there will be no one here to let you in.'

'No problem, it is just that a small hiccup has arisen, I'll be finished in no time,' I assured him.

Off I went to the local plumber's merchant. Fortunately, being familiar with the area, I knew where it was and so wasted no time as mid morning was already looming around the corner. I had seen plumbers sweating a copper to lead joint and knew that I required copper pipe, plumber's metal, and tallow, along with a moleskin wiper (I bet you did not know moles had wipers) to complete the task at hand. I confidently purchased the necessary items and set off back to complete the job.

As I said, I had seen the job done many times and it looked easy enough. so off I went into the loft whistling away. I steadily cut the lead pipe through, belled out the cut ends and inserted the copper pipe ready to tee joint the copper pipe into. Melting the plumber's metal, with my blowlamp, and inserting it, along with the tallow to the joint I wiped a reasonable looking joint. Proud of myself for this milestone I stood erect and watched as my newly formed handiwork fell onto the loft floor. Undeterred I tried again, only for the same thing to result. Again, and again the plumber's metal refused to adhere to anything except the loft insulation, no matter what I tried.

House lofts are unpleasant enough places to be in the height of summer at the best of times. The heat, coupled with the insulation floating around, causes intense itching, sneezing and profuse sweating.

Couple this with the panic that was by now starting to set in and the sweat was pouring out! I knew that the dehydration would not be replaced with a nice cup of tea made by the lovely lady of the household, as I had the water turned off – with little prospect of it coming back on soon by the look of it. After multiple attempts, I had to admit that this was not as easy a task as I at first thought – I found out later that even most plumbers are not able to carry this out as it is apparently it is an art form in its own right. An art form that is no doubt dying out fast now, as fittings are now available to fit on to any lead pipes that still remain in use.

Reluctantly I crept stealthily down the stairs, desperately hoping everyone was occupied elsewhere, only to be confronted by the proprietor, wondering when he would be able to have a cup of tea to go with his sandwich for lunch.

'Oh really! Is it that time already? I must have lost track, working merrily away.'

'Everything going alright?' he enquired.

'Well, I have hit a small snag, but it will soon be overcome. Could I please use your telephone?' I crawlingly replied with a big smile on my lips and my buttocks firmly clenched.

'Sure, but do not forget we are going away tomorrow.'

Of course not, everything will be hunky-dory soon enough. Who or what in heck was a hunky-dory, apart from being an album by David Bowie?

I telephoned the office and explained my predicament, quietly to *"His Obeseness"* lolloping in his oversized chair behind his desk, hoping that the punter would not hear the consternation in my voice. In fact, whispering and hoping that he would not hear me at all.

'Well, cutting the lead pipe was your first mistake! If you had drilled a hole into it, you would have had only one tee joint for a start.' stated *'His Enormousness'* sanctimoniously.

Realising he was right but a bit late with this gem of information, I asked what I could do to rectify the situation.

'Do not mess about anymore, just ring a plumber and get him to do it. It is your only hope. By the way, you will have to pay him yourself.' Well, no surprise there then.

'Okay, I will do that, thanks for your help,' I conceded, sarcastically.

Fortunately, the Yellow Pages was to hand, and I speedily turned to the plumber's pages. Ringing every plumber in the book takes some time, a fact not unnoticed by the house's owner, who kept popping his head around the door every ten minutes.

'Nearly sorted now,' I kept repeating unconvincingly, as every plumber in the land was too busy and could not possibly make it before the next day. Obviously, this was out of the question, as the problem needed to be addressed immediately – if in fact not sooner.

Eventually I exhausted the list of plumbers and with utter dread telephoned *His Grossness'* again. I explained to him that I had more chance of Shakespeare appearing than a plumber and enquired if he had any other pearls of wisdom.

'Right, the only chance you have got left is to go to the plumber's merchant, again, and buy some sticks of solder and a tin of flux and solder the joints together,' he snarled. 'And if you cannot finish the job today, you will have to go back tomorrow and finish it at your own expense.'

Funnily enough I had failed to mention the bit about the punter and his family going on vacation and decided that this was probably not the time to do so. Thanking him profusely for sharing his secret information with a lowly minion such as myself I replaced the receiver, dried my eyes, changed my underpants, and sallied forth on my errand.

After more expensive shopping and with time flying by, I returned, only to be met by an irate, scowling customer who obviously had little faith left in my ability.

Smiling my way past, I assured him that the problem was nearly fixed. If only I could have believed my own words, the sick feeling in my stomach might have subsided a little.

Hurrying up into the loft I lit the blowlamp and soldered the joints as instructed. It seemed to work although it looked incredibly messy, and I was in doubt as to whether it would hold the pressure of the water. But I had no alternatives left and had to pray to Poseidon that he would smile down on an undeserving subject who had learnt a valuable lesson that day.

The main stop valve was in the cellar so once I had cracked it open it was up two flights of stairs, up the steps, into the loft in about three seconds flat. Would it hold or was a great flood going to wreck the house just in time for their holiday?

Standing in the loft, holding my breath I watched as drops of water cascaded onto the insulation. Despair almost overtook me. I was ready to plunge my head into the cold-water tank. A fitting end perhaps, to a brutal day. Goodbye cruel world!

It was only then that I realised that it was no more than my tears of joy falling. Yes, it appeared that it was indeed working okay.

More speedy trips up and down to the cellar ensued as I gradually increased the pressure to its zenith. All seemed well and I carried on with the rest of the installation, constantly watching the bathroom ceiling, waiting for a damp patch to appear.

Eventually I instructed the proud new owners of the shower on its workings. Standing there in their pyjamas, clutching their cups of cocoa, and waiting to retire to bed, in anticipation of an early start next day, they did not seem overly pleased. Funnily enough I was not too surprised when the satisfaction note was not forthcoming and the only tip that was offered was, 'Never eat yellow snow'.

So, the day ended for me, driving home in the dark, having earned half the pay for one job – a lesson learned the expensive way.

I never heard if the joints held out okay. I hoped and prayed that they turned off the water before going away, but was reluctant, under the circumstances, to suggest that this may be a good idea. By the time they returned from holiday, the company and I had parted company – acrimoniously.

*

I was young and naïve at the time and left with them owing me a small fortune in owed wages. Fortunately, like everyone else employed by them I had plundered the stores before leaving and was fitting showers, for my own benefit, for many months to come and managed to regain at least some of the money I was owed.

I unfortunately did not have the foresight that at least one of the lads had. I heard shortly after I had left, that someone I knew well, and had worked with on occasions, had gone into the office on the previous Friday night. Everyone knew that 'The Blob' left early on Friday in order to exercise his right arm in the bar of his local, leaving his poor secretary, Pauline, to fend off any irate workers that ventured in after a bad week, as well as answering the telephone to all the unsatisfied customers. It was a perfect time to vent the weeks pent up fury.

Walking in, Joe (who was built like a heavyweight boxer crossed with a brick outhouse) had it all worked out. He had had a hard week's graft, but it had fortunately, on this occasion, resulted in him collecting a large amount of cash.

Striding into the office with a rather large grin on his face he said, 'Hi there Pauline. Right, there are the job sheets for this week, finished or otherwise. There is a list of money owed to me for all the half wages I have been paid so far. There is a list of money owed for this week's work – in full. And there is the balance of the money I have collected (all five pounds of it) after I have taken what is owed to me. Have a nice weekend! Oh, and by the way, could you tell 'The Fat Dickhead' that his van will be on my driveway, with the key on the front wheel, any time he wishes to collect it. Incidentally, he may want to bring his own petrol, as I will be draining all of mine off. You know that I paid for, with my money. And tell him not bother to knocking the door, unless he wants his teeth knocking so far down his throat, he will have to stick his toothbrush up his arse to clean them! Bye, have a nice life.'

*

It was sometimes the case that the client was present during the works being carried out and I must say that most of them were helpful and friendly. On some occasions copious amounts of tea and biscuits, even sandwiches, were normal – but some had to go that extra mile. Young women in negligees, carelessly crossed legs, clad in stockings and suspenders and carefully selected colourful language were sometimes the warning signals – but occasionally subtlety went right out of the window.

One of the *lads* whom I employed, on one certain occasion, was at an ordinary middle-class house, in an ordinary middle-class district of Birmingham, to carry out an ordinary small job in one of the bedrooms. Andrew, a quiet, unassuming, and quite naïve lad had been dispatched to carry out the aforementioned project before joining us others on site, across the opposite side of Birmingham.

Upon entering the premises, he was shown what was required, by a young couple who for all the world seemed *'quite normal.'* They were both around their mid thirties and although, according to Andrew, the wife was *'a little on the plump side,'* - his words, not mine – she was not fat, and indeed was quite attractive and very curvy in all the right places.

When asked if he wanted a cup of tea before he started, he gratefully accepted. Whilst Andrew was sitting at the table in the kitchen, the husband announced that he was going off to work and would leave him in the very capable hands of his wife.

'No problem, it is only a small job, and it should not take too long anyway,' Andrew said.

'Don't worry darling, I will look after him,' said the loving wife, kissing him goodbye and waving him off to work. 'Right, I will leave you to it, I have things to do. Finish your tea and just carry on as normal. I will try not to distract you too much.'

After finishing off his tea, Andrew made his way up to the bedroom, whistling merrily and thinking of his forthcoming holiday with his girlfriend. Any thoughts of holidays were soon dispelled though upon entering the bedroom. Andrew was grasping his tools (his toolbox!) in his hands as he opened the door to be met by a sight that almost caused his toolbox to drop to the floor and another tool to rise rather rapidly.

Lying on the bed, dressed only in a frilly, black and red basque, and black lacy stockings, was the wife of the establishment. Between her legs was what appeared to be an instrument of torture, humming merrily away (obviously it did not know the words) whilst she writhed around in agony, or was that ecstasy – poor Andrew unable to distinguish one from the other at that particular moment in time.

His tools were soon joined on the floor by his jaw as he agonized over his choices. He knew that he should either turn around and run out to save the young lady's modesty, or alternatively dash over and remove the offending appliance to save her from any more pain. Oh, to be so young and naïve! The former choice seemed impossible as his feet had grown roots that had penetrated the floor and left him immobile. The second idea evaporated as he realised that the way she was smiling at him and releasing deep sighs, there was no pain involved, only immense euphoria.

'I'm so sorry,' Andrew dribbled. 'I thought this was the room I had to install the socket in,' as he bent down and picked up his toolbox to hide his embarrassment.

'You do not have to be sorry. Oh, by the way is that a screwdriver in your pocket, or are you just pleased to see me?'

Placing a handful of tools in front of another quite obviously excited one, Andrew tried to turn and leave the room but found himself unable to instruct his eyes to follow him.

'You do not have to leave; you have not done the job yet,' she drawled seductively.

'B-but I-I sh-should c-come back when y-you have f-finished,' stuttered Andrew.

'That will take a good while yet, I've only just got started. Please ignore me and carry on with your work. My husband will not be very pleased if he comes home and finds the job not done. I might even find you some extra work, for which you will be well paid.'

A sweating, dribbling, shaking electrician is not the best candidate for installing a new power point, involving live electricity, especially one that is having trouble bending over and can only occasionally glance at the job in hand. Eventually another job in hand became necessary and Andrew apologised as he went to leave the bedroom.

'Where are you going?' enquired the writhing mass on the bed.

'I need to go to the toilet to relieve myself,' he replied, not entirely quite sure what he meant himself.

'If you come over here, I can relieve you,' snarled the seductress.

I will not go into the lurid detail that Andrew treated us lads to when he eventually deemed to grace us with his presence.

'Where the f**k have you been,' I shouted as he entered the site in the middle of the afternoon 'And why are you walking like John Wayne after getting off his horse?'

We all sat enthralled, as Andrew gave us a blow by blow (no pun intended) account of what had happened before he eventually finished the job – the power socket that is! True to her word, the lady had paid him for his performance, as well as the fee for the original job.

It was only as he was leaving that Andrew had the foresight to ask about the consequences if her husband found out about what had happened.

'Don't worry about that, it was partly his idea. He set up the camcorder in the wardrobe before he left but you were probably too busy looking elsewhere to notice it. He will edit the film and make copies before selling them to his mates at work. He will make a good profit on what you have been paid and I certainly enjoyed it. By the way, if anyone asks, I will give you nine and a half out of ten. Thanks for everything and if you are ever around this way again, please pop in for a cup of tea or something. I might even slip the same substance in it for you again.'

For weeks he was a pain to be around, as he told everyone he encountered about his little adventure (except his girlfriend apparently). The old saying must be true – that it is the quiet ones you must watch – although I am not sure that I would have wanted to watch him.

Isn't jealousy a terrible thing!

*

Other houses held secrets of another sort. Some had secrets that were never intended to be unearthed, but circumstances prevail to the contrary sometimes.

A certain tradesman, that I used to work with quite frequently, had a rather uncomfortable experience one day, and I will borrow and share his story with my readers as part remuneration of what he still owes me – yes, that one again. I will not put a name to this individual as he still owes me the money to this day. Having said that, I would still be willing to have a whip round for him, as and when his parents get married.

One day X was instructed, by the builder in charge of a house extension, to go to the premises and provide the heating and the hot and cold water to the newly built premises. The builders had erected a new kitchen and dining area to the rear of the premises on the ground floor only. The house belonged to a rather rich, well known, and influential professional gentleman and his wife, in a very well to do area – posh buggers.

Given that there would be no one at home, the builder gave X the key to the rear door, along with the number for the gate, a drawing, and a list of necessary requirements to be carried out – most plumbers require things to be spelled out for them. Off he went, happy in the knowledge that this would be an easy enough job carried out at a good price.

Upon arrival at the premises, hidden up a long driveway, behind a large substantial gateway and numerous well coiffured trees, he opened the house and surveyed the new extension that was nearly as big as some people's houses. Examining the new building and marking off in his head the requirements, he was happy that he could bring the necessary pipe work from the existing building quite easily. Removing his boots, he made his way through the deep pile of the cream-coloured carpets of the house. Hiding away all services as much as possible was a prerequisite of any project, and with this in mind, he explored the house from top to bottom. Deciding that the nearest connections would be in the master bedroom en-suite he returned to the van to fetch the tools and materials that would be required.

*

For the information of anyone not in the building service trades I would like to point out the following: the reason why tradesmen seem to sometimes give a very costly quotation for work in domestic premises is simply because it is more often than not *bloody hard work*. Let me quantify this as a lot of people will think I am exaggerating.

Imagine the average three-bedroom semi-detached house with four or five occupants that needs a re-wire. Simple enough, on the face of it, isn't it? It can be carried out easily enough by one man working on his own can it not? Until the following scenario, which occurs more often than people would realise. Because the cables must go from room to room, it is necessary to prepare those rooms. So, in goes the electrician and moves the furniture over to a position which will allow him to lift the floors in the places needed.

Next, the carpets must be lifted in those places. If professionally fitted, they must be lifted in such a manner that they will go back looking almost as good as when the carpet fitter left. If it was a DIY job, they are sure to be fixed down with enough nails, tacks, staples, glue and whatever was at hand at the time, to open a small hardware shop. Eventually, after working up a sweat only comparable to sitting in a sauna, surrounded by naked, nubile girls for an hour, and gaining a hernia, the carpets are lifted.

Often at this stage it is revealed why that insignificant looking carpet felt so good to walk on – the old carpet is still in situ underneath it. More sweat and a double hernia, along with permanent back damage, discloses the linoleum that was laid in the 1930s (please let it not be glued!!). Up comes the portions of linoleum that had adhered to the floorboards, due to the heat in the house over the last number of years, to at last divulge the actual floor.

Now at this point one of two things can normally be revealed. Either the floorboards in pristine condition, that will have to be treated reverently, so that they will go back after, seamlessly and without squeaking. This means cutting off the tongue that fits into the groove of the adjoining board, removing the rusty nails that have been reliably doing their job since Adam was a lad, and then lifting the boards, which are tinder dry and therefore refuse to be moved without splitting and breaking.

Alternatively, the plumber has been there before you to install the central heating, yes, the same central heating that has dried out the floorboards, cemented the linoleum, and necessitated the gluing of the carpets to ensure that the nails previously used do not penetrate the pipe work recently installed. Invariably the aforementioned plumber – or heating engineer, as some of them insist on being called – has precisionally extricated the floorboards with the use of a crowbar, an old screwdriver, a bit of old pipe and anything else that comes to hand.

This is due, in part, to not being able to recall where the proper tools are – plumbers are surely the messiest tradesmen ever invented. One can immediately tell when they are on site as every room has a scattering of tools, pipe, fittings, and other paraphernalia, regardless of if they have any work to do in that room or not.

The poor electrician is then faced with a mixture of splinters, carefully resembling an intricate jigsaw, that once removed will never return satisfactorily. Furthermore, if this devastation is seen by the client, they will not only view the electrician as an absolute cowboy but will usually insist on new boards being procured at the electrician's expense.

A repeat of this process in all three bedrooms, the bathroom and the landing eventually brings the poor broken backed, ruptured electrician to an image of a gibbering idiot requiring instant re-hydration. But at least he can now start installing new cables (after drilling all the floor joists of course). After fetching the first roll of cable from the van he glances at his watch. This reveals that it is time to start replacing the floors – and carpets – and furniture, as there is a family who have to live here tonight and do not want any inconvenience.

Yes, this is the same lovely family that has stood drinking tea and eating sandwiches whilst watching you slave away without any refreshment. The same lovely family that has insisted every ten minutes that, 'I need something out of my wardrobe,' or 'I need to use that toilet as the one downstairs is only used for storing rubbish.' The same lovely family that will trip over a lonely screwdriver or upturned carpet corner, and then be dialling the phone to a litigation solicitor before they have hit the floor. Believe me they do exist!

So, now you know why the costs are more than expected, or are even astronomical, as a polite way of saying 'Stuff that job where the sun does not shine', we can return to the tale.

*

Carrying the tools and materials onto the landing, X proceeded to move the furniture in the bedroom, in order to facilitate the lifting of the floor where the pipes were to run. When moving beds in stranger's houses it always pays to be a bit careful, as you never know what instruments or objects you may find lurking there. Upon moving the bed in the master bedroom, sure enough a motley assortment of instruments and objects were duly unearthed. Obviously, it is inevitable that one cannot help but notice what secrets are displayed when furniture is moved, be it a pile of dust and fluff or a pair of knickers long forgotten about – *here we will take a small break as you go and check under your own beds* – but on this occasion it was a variety of other things that caught the attention of X.

Picking up some of the magazines, the pages fell open accidentally – *honestly, your honour* – and a look of horror and complete shock befell the reader. X was a man of the world, having worked in all sorts of establishments, but this literature shocked him to the core. We are all entitled to our little idiosyncrasies, he thought, disgustedly, so he gathered up the magazines, the 'instruments' of various sorts, shapes, and sizes, along with the spare batteries and placed them on the bed ready to replace them to their hiding place after finishing the job.

Moving the television, the VCR, the tapes – whose titles incidentally suggested that people such as John Wayne and Marilyn Monroe were not the featured stars in them – and its table, it was noted that although this was a house with money, they obviously did not employ a cleaner. The dust lay in profusion, and when X moved anything that had lain undisturbed for a long time, he inadvertently left finger marks and streaks of cleaned areas.

'Oh well that is not my problem. I will just do the job I came to do, and they will have to clean the place after I have gone,' he said to himself.

With all the necessary furniture moved out of the way it was time to lift the carpet in order to get to the boards. Prising up the corner, X was just about to pull up the remainder of that side of carpet when his phone rang.

'Hello,' he said into the phone cautiously, as he did not recognize the number.

'Hello there, is that X,' came the reply.

'Yes, how can I help you?'

'This is Glenda, the owner of the house. Sorry to disturb you. The builder kindly gave me your number. How is the job looking?'

'Fine thanks. I should be finished today with any luck. I do not foresee any problems,' he chirpily replied.

'That is great. I just wanted to check; you have not been upstairs for anything have you? I did specify to the builder that no one is to go upstairs at all. Having those very light-coloured carpets throughout the house can be such a nuisance sometimes. As I explained to the builder, we are quite happy to have the pipe work run on the surface at low level in the dining room and we can have it boxed in after by our carpenter.'

Now X was not normally prone to stuttering, and certainly was never short of something to say – except, it seemed, on this occasion. Following a rather long pregnant pause (obviously he should have worn a condom when moving the aforementioned devices) he managed to stammer 'Er, Er, Er, n-n-no, of course I have n-n-n-not been upstairs; J-John explained everything when he gave me the k-k-k-key.'

'That's great. Sorry if it is any inconvenience, but I really do not want those carpets ruined. They cost so much money. Anyway, I will, leave you to it; I dare say you have plenty to get on with,' she said.

'Thanks, goodbye.'

Switching off the phone, X surveyed the bedroom maelstrom. 'Oh s**t, what the f**k do I do now?'

Grateful that at least he had not got any further, he replaced the corner of the *'very expensive'* carpet. Replacing the furniture was easy enough as the indentations in the deep carpet pile were very obvious. Stuffing the 'objects' and magazines back under the bed was straightforward enough as they were obviously in no particular order – he hoped anyway. After carefully replacing everything and removing all his tools, X stood back to admire his handiwork. Even from the doorway of the bedroom, the marks on the television, the VCR, the tapes, and the table, stood out like a blind cobbler's thumb.

'How the hell do I disguise that lot?' he mused.

Necessity being the mother of invention (allegedly), he knew that drastic steps had to be applied. The only way to remove the marks would be to clean the items completely. Fetching a clean piece of rag from the van, he dusted the offending articles. Apart from the pile of dust on the carpet, they did not look too bad, except for the fact that the sparkle on them belied their identity to the rest of the bedroom.

'The first thing I need to do now is remove that dust on the carpet.'

Fetching his vacuum, cleaner along with a dust sheet to stand it on, he cleared the dust away, but his former presence was blatantly obvious by the relative sheen of the television etc. There was only one way to simulate the grime that covered the rest of the furniture, and the decision was made on the spot.

Taking the vacuum cleaner downstairs, he removed the bag from inside and carefully made his way back to the bedroom. Standing next to the television, he proceeded to gingerly blow the contents of the bag over the offending components. Looking rather like a 'piper at a wedding' he stood with the bag under his arm, aiming the opening at the top of the television and proceeded to pump his arm in a slow but deliberate motion. Choking amongst the cloud of dust being emitted, he circled around to evenly distribute the muck. *Dishing the dirt'* suddenly took on a whole new meaning to him.

When he had finished, he next had to attempt to disguise the fact that he had even been upstairs. Starting in the bedroom, and slowly making his way across the landing and down the stairs, he swept the nap of the carpet with his hand in a windscreen wiper motion. Feeling like a fugitive, trying to cover his tracks, he eventually made his way back down to the new extension.

It was the best he could achieve under the circumstances, and he could only pray that the occupants would be too pre-occupied to notice the subtle changes.

Realising that he now had to start afresh, he put off ringing the builder, in order to finish the job before the owners of the house returned. It was only on X's way home that the builder in question was subjected to a tirade of verbal abuse for not passing on a simple instruction.

Nothing further was ever said about the incident, but upon the builder next speaking to the homeowners, it was stressed rather emphatically, that no one was to go upstairs at all.

It just goes to show that having money and being a pillar of society does not mean that you keep a *'clean'* house. But I guess most of us knew that, anyway, given the 'political' and 'celebrity' disclosures that have appeared over the years.

CHAPTER 11

MORE SECRETS

Sometimes little secrets were revealed willingly. One such occasion was the time when I went to a house in Birmingham, accompanied by my trusty helper, to do a complete rewire. The owners, a couple in their early fifties, seemed like a nice, normal working-class couple. The house was a normal, early twentieth century semi-detached, three bedroomed abode set in a working-class estate. In fact, everything seemed normal – until we got started.

Following the obligatory and very welcome, 'cup of tea before you start' that was about par for the course in such a property, we started on the job, taking up the upstairs carpets, floorboards etc.

As was the normal practise when these types of houses were built, there was a void under the ground floor. This would always come in useful for running the cables through and therefore I was wandering around looking for a spot that would be convenient to lift a portion of boards large enough to slip through. It was usually tight enough to crawl through, normally being between twelve inches and three feet deep under the floor and often damp and musty, but it ensured a better job aesthetically for the owners of the house – always a consideration. A host of spiders, wood lice, pythons etc. never worried a good electrician.

The husband of the establishment saw me looking and enquired as to what I was looking for. Upon informing him of the plan of action he volunteered some information.

'If you look in the rear room, just inside the door, under the carpet, there is a hatch already cut out where you can get down' he said.

'Oh thanks, that will save a bit of time,' I replied.

Following the instructions, I pulled back the carpet to reveal a carefully constructed trap door. Lifting it up I was met with a much unexpected sight. A hole had been excavated, about six feet square by two feet deep. This was lined with polythene sheet and an old carpet and contained a rolled-up sleeping bag.

My mind ran riot as I was faced with this quandary.

'It is okay, it is my son's hideout,' said the man standing behind me. 'He stays in there when the police are looking for him.'

It turns out that the eldest son of the family was a persistent house burglar. When being sought by the local constabulary, who he was on first name terms with, he and his booty would be concealed beneath the floor until such time as the heat died down.

'I know we are wrong to conceal him really, but he is our son, and we love him, even if he did not turn out quite as we had planned,' he said.

It made my life a little easier in that it was an easy access to under the floor but also presented me with a moral dilemma. Do I inform the local CID, who I am sure would be very grateful? If I do, will I be mown down in a riddle of bullets whilst walking along the road? – I had obviously been watching too many James Cagney films again. It would be blatantly obvious who had informed them if they suddenly turned up after a spate of local break-ins and proceeded to magically find the hide-away after so many previous fruitless visits. I certainly did not want a 'contract' to be put out on me – I did not charge enough for a rewire to warrant ending up in hospital or on a slab in the morgue.

When I was sworn to secrecy by the boy's parents, I knew that I could not volunteer the information, but I did manage to salve my conscience slightly. I found a gold chain and a lady's diamond ring, lying concealed away from the 'bed' in the dirt that appeared to have been dropped on the way in or out of the hole. I took them to the local police station and informed them that I had found them on some waste ground. Hopefully, someone was gratefully reunited with a family heirloom, and I avoided dying a slow painful death. I knew that I had a heart hidden away somewhere.

CHAPTER 12

RETRIBUTION?

I have often regretted not informing the police about the previous item, but things sometimes get forgotten over time, only to be remembered some years later. I know only too well how it feels to be violated by some scumbag, who sells your possessions 'down the pub', for a fraction of their worth.

Ford transit vans have always been favoured by many tradesmen, me included. Unfortunately, they are also very desired by the fraternity that would rather steal someone else's property than do an honest day's work.

Having my office at home meant that I was sometimes there during the day doing quotations or invoices etc.

One balmy summer afternoon I was sat at my desk working away when I heard the alarm sounding on my van. We lived in a large Victorian house that had a driveway between the houses leading to a rear yard, where the van was parked up. Knowing that the alarm would sometimes be triggered by a strong gust of wind I was not too concerned. However, looking out of the window I could see that there was no wind whatsoever shaking the trees and became slightly suspicious, if not overly alarmed – in fact, I was leaving that situation to the van.

It happened, that at this time, I was in the throes of building an extension on the rear of the house as well as another one on the side. This prevented me accessing the rear and side doors of the property and only left the front door as a means of going in and out. Descending the very steep Victorian stairs, I opened the front door and walked through the front garden onto the driveway.

Glancing up to where I had left the van, I was slightly bemused to see a small blue van backed up to the front of my van, which had the bonnet open and someone beavering away inside the engine compartment.

There are times in one's life when the truth does not hit home immediately and in my bewilderment, this was one of those times. I stood there thinking *'Oh; they must have come to fix my van for me'*. Suddenly realising that there was nothing to be fixed, and indeed these persons were intent on relieving me of my mode of transport, I shouted something to the effect of, 'Hey you little tinkers! leave my van alone'. I think actually that the tirade of abuse may possibly have been a little stronger than that, but it is certainly unprintable in a book of this calibre.

At this juncture, the guy who was under the bonnet, obviously intent on disabling the alarm, jumped into the passenger seat of the blue van, as his mate, who was inside the cab of my van, jumped out and into the rear. At that the van sped down the driveway toward me, driven by the ugly brute behind the wheel, obviously intent on mowing me down. I swiftly stepped backwards to avoid being killed or maimed and grabbed the handle of the rear door as the van momentarily stopped to avoid a car parked across the road. I was duly faced with another ape like moron wielding a large pair of Stillson grips and shouting, 'Come on then'. The handle of the door was then ripped from my hand as the van took off down the road at great speed and disappeared into the distance.

Being a good citizen, I rang the local police and breathlessly relayed the story in the vain hope that they would be apprehended quickly. The bored constable on the other end of the telephone drearily offered me a crime number so that I could claim on my insurance. Obviously, the flying squad were out on a desperate mission catching litter droppers that day!

I came to learn later that it is a waste of time hoping the constabulary will put in an effort to arrest such 'highflyers' as vehicle thieves. There is obviously no glory in capturing such small-time criminals and does not lead to getting one's name in the papers and a possible knighthood.

*

All this was proven to me a few years later.

I was in St. Paul's Square, a district of Birmingham, carrying out just a small job in an office, and had not even bothered taking my toolbox from the van. Pliers, side cutters and a couple of screwdrivers were all that was required and were easily accommodated in my numerous overall pockets. I dutifully carried out the repair job. Upon completion, I strolled back to where I thought I had left the van. Obviously, my memory was playing tricks on me as it was nowhere to be seen. Being a remarkably busy, self-employed tradesman, it was not unusual for my mind to be on at least another three jobs, and so I wandered the streets for the next fifteen minutes, racking my brain as to where I had actually parked it.

Eventually, the realisation that it had been stolen, filtered through my feeble mind and panic set in. I could not figure out which was the worse scenario, losing all my tools and materials; losing the van itself; or having to face the journey home on *'public transport.'*

I decided that the first thing to do was report it to the police – just in case they were interested, ha, ha – and so I walked into Birmingham city centre which was fortunately not too far away. The main police station is – or was then – Steelhouse Lane, an incredibly old Dickensian establishment that I had never seen the inside of before. Waiting my turn, amongst teary victims and various rapists, murderers, and other low life's, I eventually spoke to the person behind the desk. Totally uninterestedly he took down my particulars and issued me with a crime number, all the time looking at his watch, obviously awaiting the end of his shift. Now I realise that they are dealing with these sorts of things all day long, and have heard it all before, but to the victim it is a pretty harrowing experience – especially when they face the disturbing prospect of travelling home on *'public transport.'*

It was whilst at home, later on that night, sitting drinking tea that the reality really started to hit home. The materials like cable, boxes, clips etc. can be replaced by a visit to the wholesalers, albeit an expensive one. The test equipment that cost well in excess of one thousand pounds can be replaced, as can most of the tools, albeit again at considerable expense. But it is the tools that have been adapted for specific applications or have been in the box for too many years to remember, that can never truly be replaced. All this coupled with the fact that you are inevitably under-insured. Has anyone ever been adequately insured? Add to this the cost of renting a van, whilst the insurance company deliberately underpaid and it becomes a very costly experience indeed.

As they say in show business, the show must go on, and my business was the same. A van was rented, tools replaced as far as possible, testers ordered and materials re-stocked. The insurance forms were completed – fortunately, I had a crime number – and the working life went on and on and on.

The long wait for the insurance company to make up their minds was endured – they want to make sure that the van does not resurface before actually paying the money so desperately needed. After four weeks I never envisaged that I would ever see the van again and was pretty confident that a cheque would hit the mat soon and life could return to some degree of normality, albeit a somewhat poorer normality. Inevitably that light at the end of the tunnel gets brighter and brighter, and hopes arise, until one day you realise the light at the end of the tunnel is actually a train coming the other way.

Answering the telephone, one Wednesday lunchtime, I was surprised by the following conversation.

'Hello, is that Mr Jones?'

'Yes, how can I help you?'

'Well actually it is I that can help you. We have your white Transit van here, at New Street railway station.' Identifying himself as a sergeant at British Transport Police, he informed me that they had been tipped off by a member of the public, that three men had been seen loading metal track sections, clamps, bolts, and any other metal they could lay their hands on into a van parked adjacent to the railway sidings in another part of Birmingham.

If I wished to bring along some identification, I could avail myself of my van. After ascertaining that it was in a driveable condition, albeit only just, off I set to retrieve it – once more on public transport. I sat on the bus hoping, against hope, that at least some of the contents would still be intact.

As I walked into the station, I could clearly see my old van parked in the middle of the public car park. Anxious to be re-united with my old tub, certain that I could at least return the rental vehicle, I walked around to see how it looked. I could soon see that it looked as though it had one careful owner – followed by very many extremely uncareful ones. It looked like it had been used as a punch bag by King Kong and then driven through a jungle. There were more dents than could be counted and more scratches than I had when I caught chickenpox as a child. What is more, it was obvious that there was very little, if anything left contained inside.

Dejectedly, I climbed the stairs to the British Transport Police office and met the sergeant that I had spoken to earlier. There and then started, as far as I was concerned, a fiasco of epic proportions. A fiasco that I must relate, as I myself still find it hard to believe, even to this day.

The sergeant, who was a genuinely nice, understanding gentleman, explained that upon his constables attending the scene of the attempted theft, two of the perpetrators ran away whilst the other one just stood stock still, like a rabbit in a car's headlights. This one chap was duly arrested and brought back to New Street station and placed in the British Transport police cells. He was interviewed, as well as it was possible to interview such a low life scumbag, before he was allowed to crawl back under his stone, in a nice warm cell where he received three meals a day – quite probably more than he got at home.

Let me reiterate here and now that I know the police in England are, and always were under immense pressure. I can appreciate the fact that sometimes, in the heat of the moment, small matters get overlooked and the odd slight mistruth may emanate. I am sure a lot of us remember, 'The Birmingham Six' and 'The Guildford Four,' not to mention 'The Renault Five' – I said not to mention that! But dereliction of duty and downright lies are a different story altogether.

To get back to the story, the sergeant explained that the person, a spotty, ugly, little toerag in his early twenties, whom they had arrested, was a heroin addict. They put him in a cell, after interviewing him, and methadone was administered during the ensuing forty-eight hours that he was detained. Forty-eight hours of warmth, where he was fed and watered and given free drugs, all at the honest taxpayer's expense. During this forty-eight-hour period, Steelhouse Lane police station was informed of the arrest. A person there noted that the van had been reported stolen and someone would be around to transfer the little scrote to their premises in order to investigate the matter further. The sergeant, who by this time was getting quite irate, informed me that despite two further calls to Steelhouse Lane, no one bothered to even show up at all. The consequence of this was that they had to either charge him or release him. As he was standing beside the van, with empty hands, when he was arrested, all that British Transport police could charge him with would be trespassing onto private property. Considering the extremely low gravity of this offence it was not worth the time, effort and paperwork involved, and the stupid little 'smack head' was duly let out to trouble the general public again. GREAT RESULT! Little wonder that the streets of Birmingham are becoming more and more like a third world country. Well done West Midlands police on another excellent performance.

The British Transport police sergeant apologised for the lack of co-operation by the ordinary police, a fact that he was as mad about as I was. I left his office feeling let down and wandered down to rescue my van before the little shit decided it was an alternative to 'public transport'.

I limped the van home as best I could, all the time expecting to be pulled over by the wonderful West Midlands police, for driving a vehicle that looked like a left over from a Beirut scrap yard. In fact, it may well have been a perfect opportunity to vent some of my pent-up rage onto a member of the police force that could not bother, but of course that only happens in books. Hang on, this is a book – I could have included that!

Upon inspection at home, it was blatantly obvious that it would have to be written off by the insurance company. Every item of materials, tools and testers was missing. Even the jack and the wheel brace had disappeared, sold down the pub for the price of a packet of crisps, I suppose. One of the testers on its own had cost in excess of five hundred pounds, and I knew that this had probably been sold for a measly sum in order to feed someone's filthy drug habit.

*

Please do not misunderstand me; I have no problem with people putting into their bodies any substance they desire. After all it is their body, and we all have a choice as to our lifestyle. What irks me is when someone else suffers in order to pay for it! I know some people come from bad backgrounds and have a lousy upbringing etc, etc, blah, blah, blah; but that, to me (and many other clean living, tax paying individuals) is no excuse to expect other, innocent people to pay for their problems. Life is a constant matter of choices. As the old saying goes: – God helps them that help themselves (but God help them that are caught helping themselves). Perhaps if there was not so many, *'full of understanding, helpful, do-gooders,'* around, the world would be a better place!

*

On inspection it seemed that the only item left in the van was a roll of aluminium foil – either for wrapping the druggie's sandwiches, or more likely as an aid to smoking some noxious substance. Transit vans are great work horses but were never built for driving over fields and other undesirable places. Or loading up with tons and tons of 'scrap metal'. Hence the broken suspension and irreparable damage to the inside and outside of this once greatly used tool.

A telephone call was made to the insurance company in the hope that it would now speed up the process and I could receive remuneration in order to purchase another vehicle. Another call was also made to the West Midlands police, enquiring as to why no one had attended to the matter as promised to the British transport police sergeant.

'The matter will be looked into, and someone will get back to you Sir!' Or was that Cur?

No reply was forthcoming over the next few days, which were extremely busy for me, and it was Sunday afternoon before I could examine the van closely. Inside one of the rear door skins I spied an object that was easily recognizable. Carefully, without touching it, it was extricated from the door, using my brand new long nosed pliers. A used hypodermic syringe! As I knew for certain that it was not there before the van was stolen, I was over the moon to retrieve such an obviously important piece of evidence – Sherlock Holmes eat your heart out.

A quick call to Steelhouse Lane was made, my excitement bubbling over. The ensuing conversation went something like this:

'Steelhouse Lane police, how can I help?' asked a voice that was obviously ready to pass over to the next person on shift and go home.

I explained the situation – stolen van, recovered, smack heads, arrest, lack of co-operation with British Transport police, aluminium foil, used syringe etc, etc, etc.

'What would you like me to do with it?' I enquired excitedly.

'Right sir, if you would like to take it to your local police station, they will dispose of it for you,' came the reply.

'Sorry, you do not seem to have grasped the whole story very well,' I patiently explained. Once again, I re-iterated the foretold story for the uninterested person at the other end of the line. I spoke very slowly and very concisely as he was obviously of somewhat limited intelligence.

Only to get the reply, 'Yes Sir, if you would like to take it to your local police station, they will dispose of it for you.'

Gasping for air, with steam now emanating from my ears, I curtly replied, 'I do not wish to put too fine a point on this, but have you ever f**king heard of DNA testing?'

'Oh, you would not get anything from that,' replied the moron.

Unable to believe what I was hearing, I politely shouted, 'Excuse me but someone, someone who was involved in the f**king theft of my f**king van, has stuck this f**king needle in his f**king arm! What do you mean you would not be able to get anything from it?'

'That's right Sir. If you would like to take it to your local police station, they will dispose of it for you' he robotically replied. I began to wonder if I was actually speaking to a pre-recorded message.

'Perhaps I could speak to someone who has an IQ of above minus three then and explain it all again to them,' I uttered.

'Sorry Sir, it is Sunday afternoon and there is no one else available at the moment.'

It was at this stage I hung up in order to suffer a mild heart attack and kick the cat. I would have enquired as to the idiot's name in order to file a complaint but came to the conclusion that he probably did not know it anyway. As we did not have a cat, the wall stood in its place instead, resulting in physical pain for me, as well as the mental anguish I was suffering.

Come Monday morning I rang again, and this time managed to speak to a Sergeant. I explained it all again – stolen van, recovered, smack heads, arrest, lack of co-operation with British Transport police, aluminium foil, used syringe etc, etc, etc. including this time the conversation with his dim-witted colleague the previous day.

'Right Sir, I will look into your complaint, and someone will be along shortly to retrieve the needle off you,' said the helpful man.

'YEAH, RIGHT!' I thought to myself. I did not voice my thoughts at this juncture but ensured that I made a note of his name and number this time, ready for when no one turned up.

Oh yeah of little faith! Surely this is an apparition. But no, within thirty minutes a motorcycle patrol turned up, collected the needle, and took it away. I am fairly confident that what happened to it was – *he took it to his local police station where they disposed of it for him.* Another great result for West Midlands Police.

A couple of weeks went by, and nothing was heard and so I decided to put the matter, to date, into writing. I found out the name of the Chief Constable and fired off a letter to him that must have set his fingers on fire (if his PA ever gave it to him that is). I received a short note to say that he had passed it onto Inspector X to investigate. After he had passed it to someone else, who did the same, I received another letter from Sergeant Y to say that no evidence had been found on the needle. Considering that in the same letter it stated that they had in fact interviewed the 'smack head' at Steelhouse Lane, I found it extremely difficult to believe any of their downright dubious lies at all!

The attitude of the police was summed up one day when I telephoned to enquire about progress on the case (I can be so naïve at times) only to be told by the duty Sergeant, 'Well, basically it is just another vehicle theft.'

Again, unable to believe his flippancy, I lost it. 'Excuse me there is at least six and a half thousand pounds worth of my equipment missing from the back of that van (that was in fact the stuff that I could recall). I think that takes it into the realms of more than *"just another vehicle theft".'*

Again, I wrote to the Chief Constable. Again, I received a derisory reply, stating that all the matters that I had brought up would be investigated thoroughly. Needless to say, I never heard any more from them.

CASE CLOSED!

Is it little wonder that many people have no confidence in the police?

Remember again – *'The Birmingham* Six', *'The Guildford four'.* And this time I am not allowed to mention the other one.

CHAPTER 13

EXCUSE ME, MADAM!

It was whilst working in a previously mentioned hospital in Kent that another couple of incidents also occurred.

As we were installing the cabling for the new fire alarms, we made good use of the loft spaces in order to hide the cables as much as possible. Loft spaces are often a journey into the unknown and the site of many things discovered, that had been stowed away, forgotten, and never saw the light of day for many years. It is also a world that can sometimes reveal things that were not meant to be revealed.

One such instance was when I was in the loft above the building that housed the mortuary section amongst others. Great care must be taken when in lofts, as walking on the ceiling beams must be carried out quite deftly, so as to avoid poking a foot or a leg through the ceiling into the room below – both costly and potentially painful. Many are the tradesman that has been left standing with a limb protruding. The very unfortunate ones are the ones that have ended up with both legs through the ceiling, either side of a wooden joist and someone asking if he wants an ice cream to put his crushed nuts on. On this particular day I was in the loft running cables across and my assistant was below poking holes (perhaps I should re-phrase that?) ready to receive the cables. Large loft areas can be a little confusing sometimes as you can become disorientated as to your whereabouts – or even lose your way. This had happened to me at this point. Anyway, I spied a hole in the ceiling with light streaming through and peered down to see if I could figure out where I was in relation to where I needed to be.

Instead of seeing Steve waiting with a roll of cable I was confronted with a lady lying staring up at me instead. She was lying on her back, staring up at the ceiling and what is more she was absolutely stark naked. Being a curious sort of a fellow – and a pervert to boot – I took another quick peek before starting to turn away and find Steve. It was at this point that a pair of hands reached across and started to dissect the body of the woman before my very eyes.

I realised that I was obviously above the mortuary, and what is more, that a post-mortem was taking place immediately beneath me. Most people would probably have run away at this point, but I am more sensible and declined this possibility as running could bring about a likelihood of crushed nuts. I will spare my readers the morbid details of what took place over the next ten minutes, as I attempted to drag myself away, but the truth is I could not help but sit fascinated at the spectacle unfolding below. Eventually I located Steve, who enquired if I had bought him a bacon sandwich as well. He was convinced that as I had taken so long, I must have been to the canteen. I had to go down and offer an explanation for my absence at which point Steve looked aghast, went slightly green and ran off to the toilet. The bacon sandwich had obviously been forgotten.

As absolutely fascinated as I was, I must admit to being a little sceptical upon going for lunch that day in the canteen. I explained to Steve that there was no way I was eating liver or kidneys that particular day. My heart was just not in it (excuse the pun)!

*

On another occasion, we were in the maternity section of the same hospital, again installing the cabling for the new fire alarm system. I climbed the step ladder up into the loft to commence the cabling with Steve again underneath. The loft hatch which I had to climb through was situated in one of the bathrooms. As Steve would need the step ladder, he folded them up and took them from the bathroom leaving me stranded in the roof space.

We ran the cabling round and I told Steve to replace the steps, and I would tidy up and see him back down at the storeroom before going to lunch. I stealthily made my way back to the loft hatch and was just about to step out of the loft and onto the step ladder, when I realised that not only was the step ladder not under the loft hatch, but standing there instead, in all her naked glory, was a young mother who had just undressed and was waiting for the bath to fill.

I just about stopped myself from falling out of the hole and into the bath. As quietly as possible I crept away from the loft hatch and pondered my next move. Carefully I made my way along the loft, hopelessly searching for another way out or a way to attract someone's attention. By this time Steve seemed to be conspicuous by his absence. After searching aimlessly around for ten minutes I warily made my way back again to the opening and peered down expecting the young lady to be finished. My luck was mixed. She had decided to lay back and have a soak, but fortunately she had also closed her eyes, as otherwise she would have been looking straight up into mine. Pervert as I am, I could not stay there, as nice a sight as it was, and I again crept away.

I sat down on a board that I had found and let my imagination wander for the next ten minutes. Again, I went back, sure that she would have finished. Sure enough, she had finished and gone – Hallelujah!

Unfortunately (or fortunately, whichever way one could look at it – and I did not – well not for long anyway) she had been replaced by another young, nubile, and very naked lady, ready to have her bath. This was almost too much to bear, and I must admit I stood there not knowing whether to say something or skulk away again. Chivalry is still the better part of valour, I decided, and once more I tiptoed away. Not knowing how long the queue was for the bath, I could only wait out the time and hope that Steve would come looking for me thinking that there was a problem.

After about one hour I was not only getting hungry, but I was also in need of using the loo and once more approached the hatchway. Lo and behold, the bathroom was empty, probably because it was in the middle of lunchtime, and everyone was enjoying their food – well as much as people enjoy hospital food anyway.

More time passed whilst I sat crossing my legs and massaging my growling stomach. Whilst the absence of anyone in the bathroom meant a chance to escape, unfortunately it also meant that there was no one to replace the step ladder, in order for me to climb down again. Shouting did not help as no one answered and so I sat waiting for someone to come along. Eventually another young lady came into the bathroom and was just about to hitch up her nightdress and sit on the loo when I said, 'Excuse me but could you help me please?'

With a blood curdling scream and a comment about some perverted bloody ghost in the bathroom she shot back out of the door, knickers around her ankles, not in need of any laxatives, only to be replaced moments later by the ward sister.

Looking around she said, 'Hello is anyone there?' I thought she was taking part in a séance at first until it dawned on me that she was looking for me.

'I'm up here,' I replied hesitantly.

Looking up at me, sat in the hatchway, legs dangling, she enquired as to what the bloody hell I was doing there.

'If you would be so kind as to find a step ladder and position it underneath me, I will gladly climb down and explain all I replied. 'Hopefully, there is one parked outside the door.'

The very kind, if surly looking, sister, did as requested – the steps were indeed leaning up the wall outside the bathroom, where Steve had abandoned them – and I duly escaped the confines of my heavenly prison. I explained what had occurred, and how careful I had been not to spy on anyone or cause any embarrassment, only to get a dressing down by her for my actions. I was given strict instructions that next time I went up in the roof I was to leave a notice to that effect, somewhere visible to anyone needing that particular bathroom and notify the member of staff in charge. Sometimes you just cannot win at all!

To add insult to injury I looked for Steve – after a visit to the Gents – only to find him having a cigarette in the canteen, having just finished his very tasty lunch. The very tasty lunch that I would not be getting as they had finished serving!

He explained that he had gone to replace the step ladder only to find the bathroom door locked. Unable to locate me and getting strange looks for hanging around the lady's bathroom he had left the steps and decided to have his lunch anyway, safe in the knowledge that I would eventually turn up. Some days it is just not worth getting out of bed – or is it?

CHAPTER 14

THE BIG BREAKFAST

At this point, I would like to introduce a character called 'Hoppy'. Hoppy got the nickname after an accident at work that left him with a permanent limp. Almost everyone on construction sites has a nickname at some time or another. Some are quite polite, some are not quite so polite, and some are downright unrepeatable, but that is life on site!

Hoppy had an insatiable appetite for food. Food of any sort. I swear he only worked in between eating, instead of the other way around. Then again, he had to work hard in order to take home enough money for his wife to fill the car with food each weekend. It is said that they would have shopped online and had it delivered but neither Tesco or any other retailer had a delivery truck large enough, His lunchbox was more like the site box, the large steel vault in the corner that held all the power tools and drawings etc, for whatever job we were on at the time. He would delve into it and produce all sorts of wondrous items to devour. Many were the times that someone had to jump up and rescue his arm out of his throat as his appetite got the better of him.

The irony of it is, that he was as skinny as a lath! Why is it that some people have the ability to eat what they like, when they like and not gain weight? I look at a jam sandwich and gain a pound in weight. Hoppy could spread the jar of jam onto a loaf and eat it without effect, except maybe a couple of farts and belches and the licking of lips, ready for more.

*

He said that he had always been the same way and indeed related the story, more than once, about when he was a small child at home. His poor mother had returned from one of her almost daily shopping trips – this in the days before supermarkets – from the local corner shop. Heaving the bags onto the kitchen table, she looked forward to a cup of tea, and a putting up of the feet for ten minutes. At this point the telephone rang and off went mother, into the hallway, to talk incessantly – as only women have an amazing ability to do – to her sister.

Upon returning to the kitchen, she proceeded to put the shopping into the cupboards. Having nearly finished this enormous task, she suddenly realised that there was something missing.

'Now where have I put that bread? I am sure that I bought a new loaf with the rest of the shopping, but it is nowhere to be seen. Now I will have to go to the shop again!'

Calling out of the back door to 'Hoppy' – who's name was not Hoppy at the time but has been changed to save embarrassment – she explained that she had to go to the shop again as she had forgotten to get bread.

'OK Mum, I will be alright here,' was spluttered out amidst a spray of breadcrumbs, emanating from behind the shed, where the last remains of the missing loaf disappeared down his gullet.

And I thought my mother had it rough, putting up with me! At least when my mum said I ate like a horse, Dad would immediately remove the nosebag and give it back to Dobbin, the milkman's horse. Do not laugh, times were hard, and plates were at a premium in our house. Growing up in our house was not easy in those days as money was very tight. One Christmas when my parents could not afford to buy me any toys, my Mum cut off the bottom of my trouser pockets to ensure that I had something to play with.

*

I feel a little guilty at this point. Having just read *Angela's Ashes* – a book written by Frank McCourt, it is pretty obvious that although times were hard for us, we had it relatively easy. It is true that there is always someone worse off than yourself!

*

Let us get back to the story: -

A whole bunch of us contractors were working in South London and residing in the same bed and breakfast establishment – the same place in fact that nearly burnt down in the 'Great Pillow Fire' talked about earlier. Breakfast was served in a large conservatory at the rear of the house and was a joy to behold. A 'full English' with lashings of tea and toast was the way to face a hard day's work in those days. It was normally needed to soak up the alcohol after a night on the lash.

There was no waste for the landlady to clear away anytime as Hoppy cleared anything from anyone's plate as soon as they had had enough. In fact, I think his plate was not placed in the dishwasher but just put ready to re-use, as the only thing left on it was the pattern.

We were obviously not the only occupants of the establishment as various sales reps., office workers, and other contractors etc, came and went on an almost daily basis. Hoppy, not being a fussy type of guy, would willingly clear up after any other guests who dared to leave as much as a baked bean on their plates after vacating their tables. He really was the human equivalent of a garbage can.

On one occasion, a suited and booted guy, probably a sales representative, or someone of that ilk, arose from the adjacent table and left the dining room. He had also left half of his breakfast – much to the pleasure of Hoppy – who, with that gleam in his eye, did no more than reach across and pick up the man's plate. After scraping off the contents onto his own plate – thankfully not licking

115

the other plate clean, he returned it to the other table ready for the landlady to clear away. The remains were then duly dispatched to the waste disposal unit in Hoppy's stomach at a rate that defied belief. Washed down with another mug of tea and finished with an almighty belch, Hoppy was ready to face work – at least until morning break time, when the human vacuum cleaner could devour the next feast.

Just as we all stood up to go, back in walked the guy who had left the breakfast! Engrossed in his daily newspaper, which he had popped across the road to purchase, he walked back to the seat he had vacated and sat down. Setting down his paper he picked up his knife and fork, looking anxious to recommence his breakfast. Staring ravenously down at an empty plate, a bewildered look crossing his face, he began uttering a few expletives about his missing food. We all vacated the premises rather sharply, amidst howls of laughter, before the fickle finger of guilt was cast in anyone's direction.

Hoppy made an early start to get to site the next morning, missing his breakfast and the grilling from the landlady about the disappearing food. All the rest of us vehemently denied any knowledge of the strange occurrence. As for the suit, he had fortunately moved on – probably to another establishment – where the food did not disappear as soon as his back was turned.

CHAPTER 15

BIG RON – A CALAMITY ON LEGS

Sometimes, us regular lads on site, would encounter a new face that turned out to be somewhat extraordinary. In fact, this was not an altogether rare phenomenon.

'Big Ron' – not his real name – was a perfect example. A walking disaster – not just clumsy, but unbelievably unlucky to boot. If something on site, where Ron was working, went wrong, Ron was usually at the epicentre of it all.

Ron, a plasterer by trade, was also a jobbing builder, taking on small projects in order to eke out a living. To say that Ron was a big lad would be akin to saying that the Pope is catholic. It did not matter where you were working, if you were in the same room as Ron, then Ron was next to you. His wife and kids had insisted that he had his ears pierced, so that they could watch the television when he was sitting at home. Having said that he had a heart the size of a bucket and would do anything for anyone – a trait that often landed him in trouble on site. He was also a damn good plasterer. But unlucky – that is a vast understatement. Ron could slip on a banana skin and go arse over breakfast time even before anyone had eaten a banana!

Some of the tales that he related about himself were enough to keep the bar busy on many nights and indeed men have been known to fall from their bar stools with uncontrollable mirth. Then again, falling from a bar stool can, and frequently was, caused by a degree of inebriation – I know, I was that soldier.

*

I recall the tale, told to us by Ron, one wayward night, about the time he was building an extension on the rear of a house, for a little old widow. Said old lady had an awfully expensive, grey and white cat, of extremely rare and exotic breed, that she absolutely doted on. Many was the sunny afternoon that she could be seen sitting on the lawn, at the rear of the house, carefully dipping small shards of bread into a saucer of milk and feeding them to Tiddles. After losing her husband some ten years before, she had purchased Tiddles, at great expense, and he was now her constant companion whilst she was at home.

As the job progressed so did Ron's dislike for the lady's feline friend. Always around your feet, as cats are, Ron's rather large middle region prevented him from seeing it and he was constantly being tripped up by his newfound friend.

One particular day, knowing that the lady in question would be absent all day, due to a hospital appointment, Ron casually strolled onto the job around 11 o'clock. It was a bit of a blustery but sunny day and Ron reluctantly climbed up the ladder to continue laying the flat roof. He contemplated going home again, as he was faced with the prospect of getting blown about by the ever-increasing gusts of wind. The decision was eventually arrived at to do a couple of hours and then have the rest of the day at home, watching the horse racing on the television. As no further work was in the pipeline at that time, there was no particular need to hurry finishing this job.

Ron carefully hauled up a sheet of decking from below and started out toward the end of the already laid part of the roof. Handling an 8' x 4' sheet of material by himself was always awkward at the best of times but given the windy nature of the day this danger was definitely multiplied. Nevertheless, Ron stepped out and was immediately taken by a particularly strong gust of wind. Acting like a sail, the decking pulled Ron toward the edge of the roof and a decision had to be made quickly. The fast-looming alternatives were to either let go or plunge over the edge and the choice was inevitable. Letting go of the sheet, Ron teetered on the brink of disaster. Twenty-four stones of blubber landing would not only have caused untold pain to Ron but would also undoubtedly have left a rather large crater in the client's flower bed, alongside registering above three on the Richter scale.

Thanking the guardian angel that was looking over him that day, Ron watched as the decking floated through the air, almost in slow motion, like a leaf on the wind. But before very long the unavoidable happened and it fell flat to the floor with a definite crash. Just as it completed its descent, Ron saw something in his peripheral vision that caused sweat and goose bumps to break out all over his body – and that is a lot of sweat and goose bumps!

Unsure that what he had seen had been real, or hopefully, just a figment of his vivid imagination, he hurried down the ladder and stepped toward the decking. Lifting the one end, his fears were confirmed. Tiddles, whom moments earlier had been lying sunning himself and lazily washing his paws, was the unfortunate target of a very heavy board. Lying splayed out on the lawn in a rather large, elongated X-shape was a grey and white cruciform figure with a tongue about two feet long protruding from its very dead mouth.

Uttering such profanities as 'oh flipping heck' and 'bother' (I think the words were a little stronger, but I do not wish to offend anyone) Ron lifted the sheet and carefully made his way back to the extension. Ensuring that no grass or other tell-tale marks were visible he placed it back on the pile and considered his options.

He knew he could not leave the cat's body lying in full sight on the lawn, as it would be fairly obvious to anyone with even half a brain, roughly how the poor creature had met its demise. There was only one way out and that was to bundle the large flat body into a black bin bag and dispose of the evidence. Said pussy was folded as best as was possible (Ron's origami skills were somewhat limited) to enable it to be deposited into a rubbish sack. Stopping by the tip on his way home, he laid the *'moggie'* to rest in a skip of builder's rubbish.

Racked with guilt, but still unwilling to face the consequences of telling the truth, Ron decided that the only course of action to take would be to bluff and lie his way through. Promptly at eight thirty the next morning he arrived at the house, only to find the owner distraught and weeping.

'What on earth is wrong?' asked Ron, firmly convinced that he already knew the answer anyway.

'Tiddles has completely disappeared. I have spent half the night looking for him, but he has completely vanished,' came the sobbing reply.

'Oh dear, I am sorry to hear that. Perhaps he will turn up later,' said Ron in his most sympathetic voice.

'But he never leaves the house or garden, ever. Where can he have gone? I think someone must have stolen him. I know he was getting old, but I still loved him with all my heart. Did you see anyone around here, acting suspiciously, yesterday by any chance?'

'Oh, I did not bother coming down yesterday,' lied Ron, grimacing. 'As you were out all day and there was no one here to make the tea, I decided to take my wife shopping instead.' He thought better than telling her that he had had a Chinese takeaway last night and perhaps that she may look in that direction for the perpetrators of the crime. It did not seem the right time to try and allay the blame on innocent parties.

'That is strange,' said the lady, 'when I asked, the neighbours said they saw your van here about mid-morning.'

Adam's apple bobbing and with a face going bright crimson, Ron stuttered *'I-I-I* forgot, I had a *m-mate* ring me and ask if I could do a s-small job for him. *I-I* came around just for a *f-few* minutes to *p-pick* up a few *t-tools*. Well, must get on with some work now, otherwise the job will never get done.'

Moving as much like a grey and white cat (a live one) chased by a greyhound, as he could, given his stature, Ron scuttled out of the room and proceeded to deck the roof, grateful that the wind had abated overnight.

Mid morning, the lady brought out his tea and biscuits and gazing accusingly at Ron asked if he was sure that he did not know anything regarding the whereabouts of her beloved Tiddles. Unable to look her in the eyes, he resolutely denied any knowledge of the disappearance and swore to keep an eye open for the animal in question.

The police were informed of the alleged theft, although I would imagine that truly little resources were expended on the ensuing investigation. A stolen van full of tools and materials did not warrant any worthwhile use of police assets, so I am fairly sure that the theft of a ball of fur would not exactly excite the local constabulary into action.

It seemed to Ron that the lady never treated him with the same reverence that she had before the incident and a couple of weeks later he knew that he would have to either confess or somehow attempt to make amends.

'A mate of mine has a cat, almost the same as your Tiddles but a female,' he lied through his teeth. 'It had kittened a few weeks back and he still has one male left. He has asked me if I wanted it, but my wife is allergic to them. I was wondering if you would like it. It is grey and white and fluffy, just like your old one.'

'You know, I think I am just about ready to welcome a new man into my life, but I fear that I will not be able to afford it as I have to pay you the balance for the job you are doing soon. As you know I am on a widow's pension and money is very tight,' replied the lady.

Guiltily, Ron muttered, 'He said I can have it for nothing as he wants to get rid of it now.'

'Well in that case, could you bring me a photograph of him, just to make sure he looks suitable?'

'Certainly, I will ring him tonight and ask him to take a picture for you. Oh, by the way I have to leave early this afternoon as my wife wants me to take her to the travel agents to book a break for us.'

Later that day Ron went to the cattery where he had located a very expensive litter of grey and white kittens, paid a deposit, and took a Polaroid shot of his prospective purchase. Upon showing the lady the following day, she exclaimed that it looked 'just like Tiddles when he was a baby'.

The kitten was delivered a few days later by Ron, still feeling guilty, but with the feeling gradually subsiding, due to having to fork out a considerable chunk of his profit from the job. The woman never found out what really happened to Tiddles, but always looked at Ron with a reproachful, but somewhat amused sort of look, from that day on.

*

One Monday morning after a weekend at home, Ron failed to turn up on site and telephone calls to his house, from the foreman on site, went unanswered. Life carried on as normal as possible, although a slight delay to certain parts of the job, were noticed due to his absence. Monday went by with no sign of his presence and Tuesday progressed. Just after lunchtime on Tuesday, in walked Ron, his face looking like a baby's smacked arse.

'Where the f**k have you been?' screamed the foreman.

'Leave me alone. I had a bit of bad luck over the weekend,' replied Ron sheepishly.

Of course, word spread quickly around the site that Ron was back and that he had met with some misfortune. Everyone was conversant with Ron's reputation for bad luck and speculation was soon rife as to what had befallen him this time. None of us could wait for afternoon tea (posh site!) in order to find out the latest saga from the walking disaster.

Tea break came around and the whole site mustered around the area set aside as a canteen. It seemed as though half of the population of Salisbury were present, many faces seeming unfamiliar and far more present than a normal gathering.

'Well, cone on then,' someone piped up from the back. 'We are not here for tea and scones you know (although if they had been available, they would have soon been demolished) what the hell happened to you over the weekend, to make you miss our scintillating company on Monday?'

'Okay, you bunch of saddoes (or words to that effect) it started on Saturday night. The wife and I (Ron was sometimes under the impression he was royalty or something) were sat watching television and having a beer when she said to me, "Fetch us some fags will you, I've just run out? And while you are at it, get a few more beers. We might as well have a session to celebrate you being home for the weekend."' Excited by the sound of being on a promise, but reluctant to leave the comfort of the marital home he pondered the situation.

'I'm not walking down to the off license. I've had a really busy week and I'm knackered.'

'Well drive down then, you idle git!' came the eloquent reply.

'I can't. I've been drinking,' stated Ron.

'You've only had a couple. And anyway, it is only about three streets away. You are hardly likely to bump into anyone in that distance. I'll tell you what, while you are away, I will dress up in something sexy and when you get back, we can have a bit of fun.'

'I was out of the door like a greyhound out of a trap, keys in hand and money in pocket. I was not about to turn down an offer like that, I can tell you. Anyway, I went and got the beers and fags and was on the way home, anticipating what was to come (excuse the pun) when a police car appeared out of nowhere and flashed its blue lights at me. I pulled into the kerb and wound down the window as a copper came ambling around to the side of the car.'

'Good evening, sir. Are you aware that you have a rear light not working? Have we been drinking tonight? Would you like to step out of the car sir?'

I immediately thought, 'Well, I do not know if you have been drinking, do I? And no, I would not like to step out of the car, I am on a promise in two minutes time,' but fortunately common sense prevented me from actually voicing the thoughts.

'I stepped out of the car just as the other half of the comedy troop joined us,' continued Ron.

'Would you like to blow into this sir?' said the second rozzer.

'Before I could help myself, I found words coming out that I knew I would regret. 'Why are your chips too hot?' Straight away I knew that it was the wrong thing to say, but a vision of my wife scantily dressed in some of her *gear* was causing my mouth to work before my brain.'

'Oh, we are a comedian, are we?' Offered the *"good cop" half of the dynamic duo.*

'Right, blow into this bag now!' Barked *bad cop,* as he offered me the plastic bag with a tube on.

'Now I knew at the time that it was the wrong thing to do, but I had for years envisaged this moment, and was unable to prevent myself from inflating the bag, followed by clapping my hands either side to burst it and saying, "Got any more?"' Both cops looked at me as though I should be committed to a lunatic asylum before bundling me into the back of the patrol car.'

'I was taken down to the police station, where I was accused of refusing to give a specimen of breath and criminal damage. I explained to the custody sergeant that I had not really refused to give a specimen and sincerely apologised for my actions regarding the breathalyser as it was just an act of impulse (I am never using that perfume again) I was truly expecting to be given a lecture and released. Unfortunately, Starsky and Hutch had other ideas. I was breathalysed again, with bad cop firmly holding on to the bag and it was just barely over the borderline, so I was duly charged with drink driving plus criminal damage for bursting the bag.'

'I was locked in a cell overnight and released on Sunday morning. Meanwhile, my wife thought I had decided to go to the pub, instead of going home to her, and then stayed overnight with one of my mates. When I pitched up Sunday morning, she was in a foul mood and refused to listen to me. It was not until Sunday afternoon when a mate of mine from the golf club, who is a solicitor, turned up and agreed to represent me in the magistrate's court on Monday morning that she sort of forgave me. Even though it was her idea for me to drive to the off license, she refused to accept that it was not my fault – and before anyone asks – no, the promise had well and truly expired.'

'Monday morning saw me and my mate, the solicitor, at the court waiting to get called in. Fortunately, we did not have to wait too long before we were summoned, and we sat there as *'PC Plod'* outlined what had happened. Next, my solicitor stood up and said how sorry I was, and all that whilst I sat there looking all forlorn, as instructed by my solicitor. The judge then sat there pondering the facts for about a minute before asking me to stand. Fortunately for me, I think the judge's promise had worked out better than mine over the weekend as he seemed in a really good mood.'

'Well Mister X, I understand you were obeying your wife's request to fetch her some cigarettes and whilst I certainly do not condone drink driving, you were very much a borderline case,' stated the magistrate.

'That is correct your honour.'

'Regarding the bursting of the breathalyser bag that was not a very clever thing to do, was it?'

'No, your honour, I got carried away in the heat of the moment and acted impetuously for which I duly apologise. I did apologise to the policemen at the time, but they were insistent that I was charged.'

'So, it appears that you have come before me for a borderline case of drink driving and criminal damage costing a few pennies.'

'Turning toward *PC Plod*, he said, "Constable, I am sure this case could have been sorted by way of a caution instead of clogging up the courts for a minor misdemeanour."'

'Swivelling back to me he looked almost apologetic as he stated, "Mr X, I do not wish to see you in my courthouse again. Please walk to the shops next time you have been drinking and try to resist the overwhelming urge to pop balloons in future. Case dismissed. Oh, and by the way constable, if you see fit to waste my time again in the future, you may well find yourself on the wrong side of my wrath. Please vacate my courtroom so that I can deal with real criminals!"'

'So, you see I would have been here yesterday afternoon, but we spent the rest of the day in the pub celebrating. Unfortunately, the wife was not amused, and I spent the night on the sofa. I guess I will have to send her some flowers before I go home next time. Who knows, she might just remember her promise after all.'

As you can imagine we were all full of sympathy for Ron – as we rolled around the floor in mirth.

After all it could only happen to *Big Ron*.

*

I think it was probably the same week that he asked the labourer to nip down the shop for him.

'Could you just pop down to the hardware shop and ask the man in there for a long weight, please?' asked Ron.

*

You may well imagine that some of the labourers that were employed were not the sharpest knife in the draw. Let us face it, *'you pay peanuts, you get monkeys'*, as simple as that! This was duly demonstrated one day when the foreman told the labourer to sweep the first-floor room of a pub we were working at.

'Anything that is lying around is to go in the skip outside,' he said.

And that is what happened – hand tools, power tools, new materials – it all went in the skip as instructed. He was nicknamed 'Bungalow' from that day forward as there was obviously nothing up top. A name he seemed to wear with pride – sad boy.

Anyway, on this occasion, off went Bungalow to the hardware shop, happy as a pig in shit, to be running errands instead of sweeping floors and cleaning toilets.

'Perhaps Ron may teach me to plaster if I do the job well,' he whispered to himself as he walked down the road. 'It would be good to make more money than at present and I would be able to order the replacement labourer around as well.'

Entering the hardware shop, he spied the owner behind the counter, tidying the shelves.

'Hi, could I have a long weight please?'

'Sure, have a sit on the chair over there and I will sort it out for you,' replied the jovial owner as he carried on with the task in hand.

Over the next hour, many people came in, purchased their items, and left, whilst Bungalow sat and looked around the shelves, amazed at the array of goods available.

Eventually, checking his watch, he started to get concerned that Ron would be annoyed with him for taking so long and politely said, 'Excuse me, will you be long now with my long weight, as I have to get back for my plastering lessons?'

'No, sit tight lad, it will be up soon,' replied the shopkeeper, struggling to stifle a little titter.

"He must be waiting for someone to fetch it from the cellar." Thought Bungalow and settled himself down again for a daydream of becoming a master plasterer, earning big money, and going out at night dressed in expensive clothes and smelling like a pox doctor's clinic.

After nearly two hours, the owner of the hardware shop finally felt sorry for Bungalow, still sitting patiently, staring into space, and dreaming of the life to come. And anyway, apart from this he was occupying the only chair and that was normally reserved for the little old ladies that came in for their weekly tittle-tattle.

'Okay son you can go back now,' he chortled.

'But I still haven't got what I came for!'

'Remind me again, what did you come in for?' said the man.

'A long weight of course! It's for Big Ron, the plasterer, so it must be important.'

'Well, you have had your long wait now.'

'No, I haven't. You did not give me anything.'

'No, you have had a long wait! That is exactly what you asked for.'

'Sorry mister, you did not give it to me.'

'F**king hell! Are you thick or something? It was a wind-up – he sent you for a long wait!'

'Yes, I know, but you have not given it to me yet,' Bungalow pleaded.

Unable to decipher who was suffering the most distress from this, Bungalow, or himself, he slowly and deliberately attempted to explain what had occurred. Eventually, tearing out his own hair and beginning to gibber like a small child he shouted, 'Just go back and tell him that I have run out of weights.'

Dejectedly, Bungalow left the shop with tears in his eyes and ambled back to the site, seeing his future career crumbling before his eyes, and knowing that the new clothes and expensive aftershave were not to be after all.

Upon entering the site, he was met by the foreman, demanding to know where he had been for the last two hours.

'Big Ron sent me to the hardware shop for a long weight and it took him a long time to find out that he had run out of them. It was not my fault it took so long. I think he may be a bit slow up there.' He stated pointing at his head.

Recovering from his hysterics, the foreman eventually managed to drive home the fact that he had been taken for an idiot and told him to go and carry in the delivery of timber that everyone was having to climb over because he had not been around.

'But I have missed my lunch break, I need to go and get a sandwich and a cup of tea,' pleaded Bungalow.

Steve the foreman said through gritted teeth, 'If you do not move that timber in the next fifteen minutes, you will not be in any need of any refreshments as your head will be parting company from the rest of your body, after which you will be collecting your cards' – he undoubtedly thought it was his birthday soon as that was the only time he ever got any cards.

Needless to say, he was not pleased with Ron.

The following day, Ron, who was working on the fifth floor of a hotel with no lift, said to Bungalow, 'Just nip downstairs and get me a lath please.'

'F**k off!' shouted Bungalow. 'You are just trying to get me into trouble again.'

'No, I am not, I need a lath of wood,' re-iterated Ron.

'Well, you had better fetch it yourself because I am not falling for it this time,' shouted Bungalow.

'Oh, come on, I am sorry about yesterday. This is genuine, I need a lath.'

'Yes, well you're not having a lath at my expense,' and off he stormed leaving Ron to walk down five floors and then back up again.

POOR RON even wind-ups backfired on him!

*

Despite his size, Ron always seemed to be able to be the first to disappear from site as soon as it was time to retire to the digs for the night. This ability was inevitably due to the desire to be the first in the bath, where he would wallow for a long time reading his book, much to the annoyance of the queue awaiting their turn. The hostelry where we were staying at the time only had one bathroom without a shower, so everyone had a bath almost every night. Many were the retributions carried out for his actions, but nothing seemed to work.

One of the favourite tricks played on him was to wait until he was fast asleep before sneaking into his bedroom. Due to his size, Ron could only sleep on his back and never seemed to turn over when in bed. The heating in the bedrooms of the accommodation was electric night storage heaters and because Ron had been given the small box room, due to his snoring, his head was quite close to the heater. After a few pints Ron would go into a comatose state shortly after hitting his bed and a brass band playing in his bedroom would not have roused him until the next morning. Consequently, someone would creep into his bedroom and turn the heater up to full before retiring themselves. Ron could never work out why he would wake the following morning with his right ear resembling a pork scratching and his immense body bathed in sweat. He always thought that the landlady felt sorry for him and would turn it up whilst he was out at work and therefore, he would not say anything to her.

*

Still these revenge attacks would not deter him from hogging the bathroom nearly every night and eventually, after many months a plan was hatched to finally teach him a lesson.

The project was coming towards an end and consequently the number of guys on site was diminished greatly compared to the height of the works. Ron had been maintained on site due to his ability to turn his hand to many of the small finishing off jobs that appeared at this stage of the works. And still he had the ability to sneak from the site to ensure he was first in the bathroom.

One afternoon, just after lunch, a couple of the lads went back to the bed and breakfast establishment where they, and Ron, were staying. Armed with only a screwdriver and a plan, they climbed the stairs to the bathroom. Removing all the screws except one – which was duly loosened – from the door bolt, and the same from the bolt keep, they then made their way back to site and carried on as if nothing had happened.

At five o'clock, the foreman stated that it was time to vacate the premises. True to form, Ron was gone like shit off a shovel, travelling down the road at breakneck speed, whistling, and looking forward to his long and luxurious bath. Arriving back, he scooped up his toiletries, book, and towel along with a bottle of beer, and disappeared to run a nice, deep, hot bath. Being a *'real man'*, bath foam or anything that may make him smell a bit sweet was dismissed with the wave of a hand. 'Good old soap and water is good enough for me,' he always stated. When the required depth of hot water was achieved, Ron settled back with his book, happy in the knowledge that all the others had not beaten him to it and would have to wait their turns.

Unsuspectingly, Ron lay in his bath, reading and occasionally producing his own Jacuzzi effects which always made him giggle like a little schoolgirl – little things please little minds. Just why he felt the need to share that little nugget of information with us is beyond me, but then again, no subject was ever sacrosanct on site.

Meanwhile, the other lads were quietly assembling outside the bathroom door, with a Polaroid camera at the ready. The idea was to pin up a photograph of Ron in the bath and an accompanying notice, behind the bar, for all to see, in an attempt to shame him into being a bit fairer with the bathroom time. The general consensus of opinion was, that although it would probably make no difference at all to Ron it would still be good for a laugh.

With a deliberate, slow, careful turn of the knob and a shoulder nudge to the bathroom door, in poured the guys with shutter clicking and flashes lighting up the bathroom's interior like a teenage disco. Ron lay there speechless for a moment, attempting to take in what was happening, until a stream of profanities, mostly casting aspersions as to the general marital status of the parents of the perpetrators, issued forth from his mouth.

Amidst great mirth and a developing Polaroid photograph, the lads vacated the bathroom, careful to pull the door closed behind them. Fortunately, the building being incredibly old, the doors in the establishment fitted where they touched. This ensured that the door remained closed, if not actually locked. Let us be honest, no one wanted to accidentally see Ron lying there like a beached whale. Regardless, Ron, swigging from his bottle, settled back to continue enjoying his book. The lads after all may have a photograph, but Ron had the bath.

Approximately fifteen minutes later, Ron could hear whispered voices and footsteps in the hallway leading along to the bathroom. Suspecting that it was some of the lads coming back for a repeat performance he decided that he would turn the tables on them and have the last laugh. Carefully standing up in the bath, beer in one hand and book in the other, he held his hands aloft.

'This will give them something to feast their eyes on over their beers tonight,' he whispered to himself as the knob slowly turned and the door gradually creaked on its hinges. Standing in all his naked glory, Ron bellowed, 'Come on you bunch of dirty old perverts, have a good eyeful.'

And have a good eyeful they certainly did.

Unfortunately, it was not any of the lads at all, but the landlady of the establishment, showing a young couple around, who had just booked in for the night.

'Now, this is the bathroom,' she started, 'a-a-a-and this is Ron, one of our residents,' the landlady stuttered.

Discreetly covering his manhood with his book, Ron, going a funny shade of crimson, slowly sank back into the water as the landlady glared, the young man looked disgusted and the young girl blushingly giggled, whilst reaching in her handbag for a magnifying glass.

Ron took solace in the fact that at least the landlady had not said, "This is Dickie Withers." After all the water was starting to turn cool by this time.

It was some time before Ron could pluck up the courage to enter the bar for his dinner. As he did so the room erupted in a maelstrom of laughter, clapping, wolf whistles and waving of the upper half of little fingers. The Polaroid photograph was already pinned up on the bar and obviously by this time the whole of the busy barroom was in on the joke.

The young lady who had had the misfortune to be a witness to the encounter was the first to speak – 'Ron isn't it? Sorry we did not recognize you with your clothes on.'

At this juncture, Ron, wishing he could crawl up his arse and drag it in after him, and quite expecting to be punched by her boyfriend, sat quietly at the bar, and ordered a pint. As her boyfriend approached, he cringed, ready for the fist, only to be surprised at the words emanating from his mouth – 'Don't worry, she was not wearing her glasses – and anyway she is a nurse and has seen far bigger and better than that.' Ron was not quite sure whether to be insulted or relieved and settled for just smiling and sipping his beer.

Whether Ron learned a lesson, even after buying a large round of drinks, is debatable, but he always carried a piece of wood around with him after that incident, to wedge the doors closed, when going anywhere that involved even partial undressing.

*

At the time that I knew Ron, he had only ever had one brand new car in his life. It was a brown Morris Marina (that shows how long ago it was) straight from the showroom – sparkling and glistening like only a new car can, in the eyes of its owner.

It was Ron's pride and joy, his baby – his wife and he had not had any kids – and he would drive the streets carefully, proudly showing off the latest addition to his family.

One day, about two weeks after taking delivery of the new addition, Ron was out heading for the shops. Fortunately, this time he had not been drinking. Unfortunately, the night before had been extremely cold and there was a danger of black ice, according to the weather forecaster on the television.

Ron was confident in his driving ability, after all this baby was the latest in modern technology. After driving various junk heaps around for many years, the many features, and gadgets (things like a handbrake and interior lights) mesmerised Ron. He claimed to have once owned a Rolls Canardly. He said it rolled downhill but could hardly get up them (sorry, that was one of my dad's).

Even though he was self-assured about his skill as a driver, he still took it steady as he did not want to take the risk of hitting the kerb or anything else and causing a scratch or even worse damage to his pride and joy. Going down a hill he slowed up even more, but unknown to Ron he was approaching a large sheet of black ice. Before he knew what was happening, the car started to do an impression of week one of *Dancing on Ice* As the car started to slew to one side, panic set in and the brakes were applied. Fear and trepidation flashed across Ron's face as he started to lose control. Remembering his driving instructor's advice, he dabbed at the brakes and drove into the skid. Eventually the car started to slow down and straighten up after what seemed a lifetime of waltzing around.

'Ha ha, you thought you had me there, but I am too good for that,' he said cockily, to no one in particular.

Just at that moment the car veered toward a lamppost. Desperately turning the wheel left and right, it appeared to drift ever closer as though in slow motion. Dabbing the brakes helped to slow the car but its course seemed to be pre-ordained. Hypocrisy can easily slip in at a time such as this and Ron, a strictly non-religious man, attempted to say a prayer to a higher entity.

The praying was in vain as the car lined itself up with the lamppost, head on and dead centre.

Fortunately, the dabbing of the brakes had had sufficient effect to slow the impetus of the vehicle and Ron could do no more than sit and watch as the car impacted against the mortal enemy. Fighting back the impending weeping, he opened the door and stepped around the front of the car in order to inspect the damage. Being a fairly sturdy model of car and having no rust or weaknesses yet, he was over the moon to note that although there was a small indentation in the chrome bumper, there was no damage to the rest of the bodywork. Tears, a mix of sadness and elation welled up as Ron re-entered the car.

Through a mist in his eyes, he put the car into reverse and turned his head in order to vacate the area before anyone he knew should behold his plight. Slowly reversing, he had only gone about a foot when there was a strange creaking sound followed by an almighty crashing noise. Looking forward again he could see that most of the lamppost was obvious by its absence. At this point it pivoted forward again to scrape down his bonnet after denting the roof. Unable to hold back any longer, he let forth with a flood of tears as the cast iron object continued to slide to one side defiantly removing his wing mirror in the process.

Devastated, Ron backed up and drove home, leaving the lamppost lying in the road, to show his wife the slightly remodelled car with the sagging head lining and only one wing mirror.

'Never mind,' said his wife consolingly, 'the insurance company will cover the repairs. We will just have to find the excess to pay.'

'Sorry to remind, you but if you remember, after we paid for the car, we could only afford to insure it third party, fire and theft,' said Ron through his blubbering.

Referring to Ron as an idiotic son of unmarried parents – or words to that effect – she chased him around the house with a rather large kitchen knife attempting to turn him into a eunuch before he managed to escape out of the door and down the pub to drown his sorrows.

Two weeks later he felt like drowning himself instead, as to add insult to injury he received a bill from the council for a new lamppost. Apparently, he had been seen on CCTV and the authorities had traced his address through his number plate.

Such is life for our Ron, I am afraid, bless his little cotton socks – even if they do smell like six-month-old gorgonzola.

CHAPTER 16

DON'T BLOW A FUSE;
IT'S NOT WORLD WAR THREE – EVEN IF IT DOES
SOUND LIKE IT

As I have mentioned before, working away from home was normal and sometimes it was necessary to try and save some money on the accommodation side.

Many are the nights I have spent curled up in a sleeping bag in the front of the van, in the rear of the van or even on a floor somewhere. Sometimes this was because accommodation was hard to find, sometimes for sheer convenience and sometimes, more than likely, through pure financial restraints.

Being self employed is not always the lucrative life that some people envisage. Yes, when times are good, the work is available and the money is rolling in, life can be relatively good – although only in return for a fair (or even sometimes unfair) amount of input. But when the money is being withheld deliberately, or a customer has gone bankrupt, leaving you owed thousands of pounds, life can be extremely difficult, believe me.

*

I remember when I was doing a job somewhere in the north of England one time at a supply warehouse. It was at a time when a builder that I had done a lot of work for had gone into liquidation –

owing me a great deal of money that would never be forthcoming. I had already laid out thousands of pounds in wages, accommodation and materials and still faced big bills for further materials bought on account. Because of these facts, staying in bed and breakfast at this time was out of the question, and after spending one night across the front seats of the van, with the gear stick acting like a gay man on heat every time I turned over, the prospect of another night of being probed and prodded was not top of my wish list.

After a word in the establishment manager's shell like, he agreed that I could sleep on the office floor, on the proviso that I was up and working before anyone came into work the next mornings and no signs were left of my habitation. Oh, such luxury – a carpeted concrete floor, a sleeping bag, and my coat for a pillow – yes having your own business can be really good at times!

I worked until about midnight, punctuated only by a break for a cup of tea and a sandwich that I had bought earlier. Having not had a great night the night before, I settled into my sleeping bag and immediately dozed off into a slumber filled with dreams of cables, lights, and other electrical paraphernalia. Okay, so it may have had nubile, scantily dressed young ladies doing wonderful things to my body, but I am not about to share those sorts of things with the likes of you!

In the early hours of the morning, with my body by now suffering the aches and pains associated with lying on a hard-concrete surface, my dreams were rudely interrupted by noises emanating from outside the factory unit. Probably nothing more than kids setting fire to the building, I assured myself and set about rescuing what was left of the night's much needed sleep. Unable to smell smoke, I drifted back to the land of my nubile friends, certain that all my aches and pains were soon to be massaged away by their capable hands.

How long had passed I am not sure, but through the pleasure I was receiving I became semi-conscious of more noises, quieter but perhaps closer than before. I was at a crucial moment in hand, in the dream, if you get my drift, and unable, or at least unwilling, to lose it all by waking. Suddenly there was an explosion of light as the dream climaxed.

'What the f**k are you doing?' thundered a voice from above. Had I had the calling? Was there a supreme being summoning me to higher things? Surely not with such profanity!

Now I do not know if you have ever been brought to earth, by a loud voice, in the crucial moment of a lovely dream, whilst completely enveloped in a sleeping bag that is determined to do an impression of a roll of cling film (yes, I saw that film too). But believe me, it is not funny at all. At least not to the person enveloped and desperately attempting to free at least his arms, in order to protect himself from what is obviously an intruder intent on doing dark things to his being. At least that is what ran through my mind in that split second where the nubile ladies all ran off, only to be replaced by an ugly, bearded, knife wielding sceptre.

Nimbly jumping to my feet, I was immediately returned to the floor by the all shrouding sleeping bag whilst my sadistic attacker stood over me ready to strike the final death blow.

'Don't hit me! I can explain,' I snivelled, whilst getting to grips with the zipper on the sleeping bag.

'Oh, can you smell that awful smell?' he asked.

'Smell it. I'm f**king lying in it.' I ventured desperately attempting to free myself from my constraint.

I eventually wriggled out of my captivity and stood poised ready to do my impression of Bruce Lee. I can only guess that the sight of me standing there in my underpants was not really that stirring, as he eyed me from head to toe like something awful that he had trodden in. I was only glad at this time that the shock of being so rudely awakened had caused my dream filled excitement to leave me.

'The manager agreed to me having a short kip on the floor as I was working late,' I said.

'Oh, that's alright then. I'll get on with my delivery and leave you to it,' he replied.

It turned out that this branch of the company, along with all their other branches, sent in their orders at the cessation of business and the warehouse then delivered overnight ready for start of business the next day. An efficient method of working but one that I wish the manager had shared with me beforehand.

After a satisfying cup of tea and a biscuit he went on his way, after agreeing to not mention my presence to anyone else.

Me? I just congratulated myself on my bravado, faced with the situation, and tried to get back to sleep, but the adrenaline was still coursing through my veins (makes a change from alcohol I suppose). After another soothing cup of tea, I decided that an early start was probably best anyway. After all, the sooner this job was done, the sooner I could move onto the next one. Who knows, it may have a deeper pile carpet?

*

To return to the subject of WWIII, this occurred in a place called Haydock in the north of England. Situated between Liverpool and Manchester, it is probably most famous for its racecourse, which was just up the road from the industrial estate, where the company I worked for had wired all the lighting and power etc. in a large warehouse. The lads that had actually carried out the job had clubbed together and purchased a caravan to live in during the three-month duration of the project. The expenses paid by the company had eventually paid for the caravan, and after that they were in profit, and looking forward to re-selling said caravan providing they could find someone with *mug* tattooed on their forehead.

I had to go up at the very end of the contract in order to carry out a few items of snagging and extra works, as the lads that did the original work were all tied up on another major project – probably tied up by the foreman to stop their antics. Meeting one of the lads on the Monday morning to get directions etc. he gave me the key to the caravan and said I was welcome to use it for the two nights that I would be there, after which I could disconnect the temporary electric supply ready to move it off site. Apparently, they had someone lined up who was interested in purchasing the 'luxury' mobile home.

Off we went, the electrician's mate and me to find the site, do the snagging works and return as the intrepid heroes of the hour.

Following our trek up the M6, we located the site and checked in at the foreman's office. After surveying the site and the work to be done, we decided to unpack our clothes and made our way over to the caravan. Not exactly five-star accommodation but we were used to roughing it. We plugged in the electric heater to air out some of the dampness before returning to the warehouse, unloading our tools and materials, and making a start on the necessary work.

We worked until about seven o'clock, then cleaned ourselves up as best we could and went off to find the nearest hostelry for refreshments. Closing time came and off we went back to our cosy mobile home. Whilst we had been inside the pub it had started raining and was merrily lashing down now – well, Haydock is quite close to Manchester, where the natives have webbed feet from the incessant downpours. We had both had a bit to drink – not drunk, but slightly inebriated – this being in the days when drink driving was not considered a real big deal. I hasten to add that I do not drink and drive nowadays – it just is not worth the risk to me and others. Pulling up at the caravan, Tommy jumped out to unlock the door – he was after all the mate, and I was quite willing to pull rank in such damp circumstances. As I watched, he placed the key against the lock and immediately sharply pulled back his arm. These movements were then repeated a couple of times more before he jumped back in the car.

'What is your problem?' I enquired. 'I give you one simple job to do and even that is too difficult.'

'I caught a pisser.' Tommy explained. "*Pisser*" is the technical term for an electric shock – well it is amongst the electrically minded fraternity. 'Every time I touched the key to the lock it happened again.'

'See, I told you not to drink so much. You are but a young boy, trying to fit into a man's world and ending up looking silly. Believe me, I have been there, done that,' I retorted.

'No honestly. Every time I touched the caravan it happened.'

'Here give me the key I will do the job myself. No good leaving it to a young strip of a boy,' I glibly said.

I jumped out of the car, slammed the door, for effect, and marched confidently up to the caravan. Touching the key, a little warily, to the lock I received an electric shock and withdrew my arm at considerable speed. I tried a couple of more times, but the result was the same each time. The car window was suddenly wound down a little and a squeaky voice, attempting to hide its mirth said, 'See, I told you so!'

It is surprising how quickly one can attain sobriety when the circumstances decree!

'Okay smart-arse, you were right, but I do not understand, everything was alright when we left it.'

'It must be something to do with the rain and the damp.' Uttered the voice of Sherlock Holmes, from inside the warmth of the dry car.

'Well done Einstein! Well, I am not sleeping in the car when this is available, so we had better devise a plan to get in and find out what the problem is,' I hollered.

After locating a roll of insulation tape in the car the head of the key was duly wrapped up and inserted, and the lock opened. Making our way tentatively into the interior, we embarked on a mission to find the source of the problem, being very careful not to touch any exposed metalwork. Eventually, after much detective work, we discovered that the cable entering the caravan, through the aluminium vent, had rubbed against the vent over time and got damaged. This had resulted in the live wire rubbing barely against the metal frame of the caravan. The damp conditions ensured a path for the electrical current to find a path through.

'I am surprised that it had not blown a fuse the other end,' I said as I pulled the cable through, exposing the problem, which was then duly taped up with the insulation tape. 'Probably just as well, because we would not have been able to get into the foreman's hut to fix it anyway, and we would have been without heat and light.'

Tommy, standing in the rain and touching the metalwork of the caravan confirmed that the problem had indeed been rectified, and we were assured that it was safe to go to sleep. It is utterly amazing what the threat of violence can achieve sometimes.

Curled up in our sleeping bags, safe in the knowledge that we would not be electrocuted in our sleep, and the effects of a good meal and a few beers kicking in, we settled down to a good night's sleep.

'Goodnight, John-boy,' whispered a little voice in the darkness, still slightly tipsy.

'Goodnight, Mary Ellen,' I replied in as butch a voice as I could muster.

A few minutes later, just as I felt myself drifting off to sleep, came an almighty '*bang*' from somewhere outside the caravan. I shot up in my sleeping bag to a sitting position as Tommy fell off the bed and onto the floor, still inside his.

'What the (hell) was that?' (Or words to that effect) a muffled voice enquired from the depths of the pile on the floor.

'It sounded like someone shooting,' I replied.

Hesitantly I pulled back the curtain and peered out into the inky blackness, only slightly illuminated by the moon, which itself was mostly obscured, by the rain clouds.

'Can you see anyone?' said a quivery voice from below.

'No, have a look on your side,' I responded.

'Bugger off, I'm not exposing myself (in itself a ghastly thought). There might be a nutter out there, intent on slaughtering us in our beds,' said Tommy.

'You have been watching too many scary films, you big baby. It is probably only somebody shooting rabbits or something.'

Eventually Tommy crawled back up onto his bed and hesitatingly squinted through a small aperture in the curtains.

All was quiet and still as we scanned the horizons for any shapes lurking around. Nothing untoward was to be seen and so, with some trepidation, we soon settled down again, listening to the rain drumming incessantly on the roof.

Again, just as I was entering the land where the nubile lovelies awaited me, there came the sound of a single gunshot. Adrenaline pumping, and the sleeping bag filling up with something brown and smelly, I was immediately jerked back to the moment. Once more we scoured the surroundings for any sign of life, only to see nothing moving at all. Just stillness prevailed.

Ten minutes later, when the same thing happened again, I was already wide awake due to lying there in anticipation.

'I have had enough of this,' I said to Tommy, who was by now lying under the table, convinced that his life was destined to end in a manky old caravan, on a rainy night in Haydock. Butchered to death, by a hairy, wolf like madman prowling around on the night of the full moon – now who has been watching too many scary films?

Opening the caravan door, I shouted in my poshest possible

'Brummie' accent, 'Oy people are trying to sleep in here. Give us a break will ya!'

'Don't annoy him,' squeaked Tommy.

'Well, we have to get some sleep somehow,' I replied.

No answer came the loud reply, as the rain continued to hammer on the roof. Whoever was out there was determined to make us suffer terribly in our last minutes on this planet. Once again, we settled down, actively listening for any slight sound emanating from the outside world.

Bang! Then nothing again.

'Right, you look out of the window on your side, and I'll look out this way to see if we can see anything,' I volunteered.

We both sat bolt upright, unable to sleep by this time, and determined to get to the bottom of what was happening.

After a few minutes there came the sound of the gun, only this time I was able to see the blinding flash of light. It was located between us and the foreman's hut at a distance of about twenty yards or so from the caravan. Staring into the night I was still unable to make out any shape or form, as silence descended. Only the sound of the rain, which by this time was increasing, made any disturbance in the stillness.

'Did you see that?' enquired Tommy.

'Sure did, but I still cannot see anyone or anything, just a bright bolt of light when the bang happened. Keep watching and if we see anyone, I am going to call the police,' I replied.

We kept watch and sure enough after about five minutes it happened again, and again after a further five minutes. In fact, approximately every five minutes following that, it was repeated. Eventually at about four o'clock in the morning, the rain slowly abated. As the rain slowed, so did the explosions, eventually stopping some time after the rain had finally ceased. At last, much needed sleep overcame us until around 10 o'clock when we both wearily drifted back into consciousness.

After dressing we drifted over to the foreman's hut, and over a very welcome cup of tea, related the night's events to him as he sat there spellbound. Then the three of us walked across the site, looking for the possible cause of the war that had happened outside the caravan. After a few minutes searching, we came across the cause – there in a rut in the ground, caused by the constant passage of tyres, lay the cable feeding across to the caravan. The outer sheath and part of the inner sheath had been damaged by being continually run over and had eventually exposed the inner wire. As the rain had seeped into the rut the water had built up and connected the cable to the earth, causing a short circuit which in turn had exploded and apparently blown the water back out.

'But why did it not just blow the fuse?' I ventured. 'That is what should have happened!'

We made our way back to the hut, after arming ourselves with some tools, and investigated this new phenomenon. Upon opening the appropriate switchgear, it was made patently obvious why the normal pattern of events had not transpired. Someone had replaced the normal fuse wire with a steel nail which had withheld the forces unleashed upon it and caused WWIII to resume.

After affecting a temporary repair to the cable – and replacing the fuse for safety's sake – we completed the jobs that we had come to do and then disconnected the caravan along with all the other temporary electrics and returned to Birmingham, leaving the caravan to be *'safely'* forwarded to its new owner.

CHAPTER 17

PICKING UP THE PIECES

On many occasions in life, things go belly up and this is also true at work as well as in other aspects of our *'normal, everyday existence'*. Numerous classic examples spring to mind and I will try to convey to you some of the more outstanding ones.

An occasion that immediately springs to mind is when I had more work to do than was good for me. This was not an uncommon experience as it is difficult, when running your own business, to turn work away when opportunity presents itself. After all, when work is scarce one is grateful for a job coming along and therefore when asked if I could fit a project in, as much as I tried to say no, it invariably came out as yes.

All the lads I employed at the time were ensconced on various jobs and I personally was firmly entrenched on a quite large public house refurbishment in deepest South Wales. Yes, that land where the men are men – and the sheep are terrified (sorry Richard)!

Anyway, I received a telephone call from a contractor that I had only carried out one small job for, but who was in a position to offer many more varied, sizeable contracts. Some other electrical contractors had let them down on a rather large nursing home extension just outside Northampton. Could I possibly step in, in a week's time and wire the extension in order for the plasterers to continue?

I knew that it was impossible, due to my present workload, without employing another pair of hands, but could not take the chance of saying no. Too much was at stake to not grasp this opportunity that had fortuitously arisen. During the ensuing conversation it was arranged that the necessary drawings would be sent by post, and I immediately commenced telephoning around my contacts to recruit another suitable electrician. After many enquiries, I received a call off an electrician, stating that he was looking for some work on a sub-contract basis and after hearing from a mate that I was looking for someone, would be interested in taking me up on the offer of some employment. It was arranged that he would come to my home on the Saturday afternoon for an interview.

Saturday afternoon arrived very quickly indeed and sure enough there on the doorstep was Nathan. He looked respectable and after a chat over a cup of tea and a biscuit (no expense spared for my employees), it seemed as if he knew his way around the electrical installation business. I showed him the drawings for the nursing home, and he seemed confident that it would not be a problem wiring it. He would be on site to commence at eight o'clock on Monday morning. I gave him the drawings, the rolls of cable and all the other necessary ancillary items he would need to carry out the job and off he went. Everyone was happy – or so I thought!

Early on Monday morning I whizzed off to Wales whistling and feeling perky and happy. Unfortunately, Perky and Happy demanded that I stopped feeling them and instead stop for a bacon sandwich. Upon reaching the pub I engrossed myself in my work, happy in the fact that everything was going well, and the money would soon be rolling in. The future looked bright.

Around 10 o'clock the phone rang, and I answered it to find a slightly befuddled voice enquiring where the electrician was on the site of the nursing home. I assured the foreman that he was somewhere on site, undoubtedly in one of the many rooms, toiling away, pulling in cables. Back to work I went only to be disturbed a few minutes later by the foreman again, informing me that a fruitless search had been carried out of the whole site and there was definitely no sign of an electrician anywhere. After placating him I rang Nathan but there was no answer. I was confident that he was surely making his way to site and would ring me back shortly. After about fifteen minutes I still had not heard from him and so I tried his number again. It went straight to voicemail and a call to his landline went unanswered as well. Unable to comprehend what was happening I rang the foreman back and informed him of what was happening and requested that he inform me of any appearance by Nathan. He was quick to point out that the plasterers were due on site the following morning and that the cables and other equipment needed to be in situ forthwith. Once again, I managed to appease him and assured him that it would be done, on time, by one method or another.

I was fortunate that the job I was on at that time, was well in front of where it needed to be, as far as I was concerned, and started packing my tools in order to return to Birmingham and sort out the obvious breakdown in communication. I could soon return to Wales when it was back on track.

Onto the M4 motorway and pedal to the metal time, the Transit was flying down a steep hill when there was an almighty banging and screeching noise emanating from the underside. Thinking the exhaust pipe had come adrift, I indicated and pulled over to the hard shoulder to inspect the damage before continuing on my journey. I was confident that it would not be anything major as I had only purchased the vehicle two weeks earlier. Upon looking under the stationary van I was aghast to see the front end of the prop shaft hanging on the floor. I realised at this point how lucky I had been as if it had dug into the tarmac, it could have flipped the van over completely.

I was obviously going nowhere in this van and whipped out my phone to ring the RAC rescue service. Then I remembered that I had told them to stick their membership where the sun does not shine, only a week earlier, because they wanted to double my premium after using the service too many times (in their opinion) in the previous twelve months. With no time to spare I had no alternative other than to use the emergency telephone by the side of the motorway to call the police. After a relatively short wait I was towed off the motorway and into the local garage. I explained my predicament to the owner and expressed the need for urgency in getting back on the road.

Upon inspecting the damage to the van, now up on the garage ramp, *Jones the grease monkey'* (that needs to be read in a Welsh accent) looked at me and gave a sharp intake of breath. A new prop shaft would be required, and it would be a couple of days before it would be repaired – at considerable expense, of course – and that was apart from the exorbitant cost of getting towed off the motorway.

Panic was by now starting to set in as my phone was getting warm from the number of calls enquiring as to when someone would be on site at the nursing home. Of course, I had no alternative but to authorise the said repairs – at considerable expense, of course – and then enquired as to where I may be able to hire a replacement van. Obviously, by now I was desperate to get away up the motorway and find out what had gone wrong.

'Oh, my brother has a vehicle rental company, not far from here, he should be able to sort you out with a van. I will give him a ring for you.'

Fifteen minutes later up rolls *Jones the rental'* (Welsh accent again please) grinning from ear to ear, driving a Peugeot nail. He informed me that he would do me a special deal for the hire, all this whilst attempting to keep a straight face. The figures he quoted were considerable to say the least, but I had no alternative but to stand being mugged by the *'brothers from the valleys'* (and once more).

Once again on the road I made my way as fast as the van would take me back to *'Brum'*. I went Straight round to Nathan's house and was somewhat dismayed to see his car parked outside. Upon ringing the bell Nathan appeared at the door.

'Hi,' he said nonchalantly.

'What happened? You were supposed to be at Northampton this morning.'

'Oh, I decided not to take the job.'

To say I was gobsmacked would be an understatement. I did not know whether to laugh or cry – or give him a swift kick in the nuts. What could I say to such an insensitive, selfish, uncaring bastard?

The best thing to say under the circumstances I decided was, 'Give me the materials and drawings, I will go there myself. I cannot believe that you had not even got the common decency to give me a ring and let me know. I have had to come all the way back from Wales for this.' He just shrugged his shoulders and led the way to his car to retrieve the stuff. No more conversation was necessary as I loaded the van, fit to blow a fuse myself.

I rang the foreman on the nursing home job and explained to him that I was on the way and come Hell or high water the plasterers would have some rooms wired and ready to go at by the following morning. Working through the night and the following day ensured that I was true to my word and within a couple of days I completed the first fix wiring on the first phase of the new build and was ready to return the hire van and carry on with the Welsh project. I wish that energy drinks had been invented in those days. As it was, I existed mainly on a diet of caffeine tablets. Not a clever thing to do sometimes as I was to find out, but needs must as the devil drives.

The van was duly returned the following day and I was presented with the news that my own van was roadworthy again, along with an invoice for the repair. They had obviously decided to fit gold plated replacement parts as this was reflected on the bill. Anticipating the likelihood of this I had robbed the children's money boxes and searched down the back of the sofa for any loose change but had not anticipated having to take out a second mortgage. After some objections and negotiating it was obvious that I would not get the keys until it was paid for and so with a heavy heart, I settled with the modern-day Dick Turpin and went on my way.

Thinking everything was at least back on track I carried on regardless. On that afternoon I was having a cup of tea and thinking about my considerably reduced financial situation. I had contacted the garage where I had purchased the van from a few weeks earlier, knowing that they had done some work on the gearbox, which would have necessitated removing the prop shaft. It was obvious to me that someone had been negligent in replacing it, but they insisted it was nothing to do with them and no remuneration from them toward the repair would be considered. I sat there feeling sad and dejected when a little voice said, 'Smile, things could be worse.' Unable to see how things could possibly get worse, I decided that it was probably the right thing to do. So, I smiled – and sure enough – things did get worse!

Tea break over, I was merrily working away, oblivious of what was to come when the telephone rang. As it turned out it was the foreman on the nursing home informing me that the second phase of the job was now ready for first fix wiring and requesting that I attend there the following Monday morning as the plasterers were once again hot on my heels.

This time I was ready though. I had received a call from an electrician earlier in the week looking for some work. A quick call and all was set. But, once bitten twice shy. There was no way I was taking the chance of him not turning up this time and arranged that I would go down with him myself and start the necessary works before leaving him to carry on. That should solve the problem before it had a chance to arise. Arrangements were made for him to be at my house at seven o'clock Monday morning. Sure enough, seven o'clock arrived and so did Barry. That was the good news! The not so good news was that he would have to leave early in order to attend college on the evening where he was taking a course. Although this would entail using two vehicles instead of one it was not a major disaster. At the very least he had turned up.

Fair enough I thought, I cannot knock anyone for trying to further their knowledge. It just meant that I would have to stay with him and probably after him to get the job on track ready for the plastering to commence the next day. We set off for Northampton in convoy, duly arriving and after showing him the site and the drawings we set about the necessary work. Barry seemed proficient and throughout the day we progressed nicely until around three o'clock when he informed me that he had to leave in order to get home in time for a shower and change before attending his course. No problem. I carried on regardless, carrying on where we had left off.

Everything was going swimmingly until I went to fetch another roll of cable from the van shortly after he had left. Standing by the van, I searched my pockets for the keys. Having good quality overalls on was a great idea until I realised once again the abundance of pockets they contained. I searched and searched but the bunch of keys were conspicuous by their absence. It was at this conjuncture that I recalled sending Barry to the van earlier for some materials. As he had not too long left, I rang him with the hope that he would just turn around and bring the keys back. No harm done; we all make mistakes – as the hedgehog said climbing off the scrubbing brush. His phone was answered on the second ring.

'Hi Barry, have you got my van keys? You fetched some stuff earlier and I think you forgot to give them back to me.'

'No sorry,' came the reply that I did not want to hear.

'Are you sure?'

'Hang on, I will stop and check my pockets,' said Barry.

Two minutes later, 'No sorry, I am sure I put them down on the side by where you were working.'

'Okay thanks I will go and have a look around, they must be inside,' I said totally convinced.

I scoured the area where I had been working. Then I scoured the area where Barry had last been working. No keys. I checked the site around the drawings, around by my toolbox, around where Barry's toolbox had been. I combed the site hut where we had our tea. I foraged the entire site, even resorting to tipping some of the elderly residents of the nursing home upside down to see if my keys fell out of their pockets. I rang Barry again, but his phone went straight to voicemail. I knew deep in my heart that he had them in his pocket when leaving site but was either too afraid to admit it or was not prepared to turn around and bring them back to me.

Needs must as the devil drives, and I needed a roll of cable from the van to carry on working. After some deliberation I bit the bullet and decided to break into the van. After two paracetamols, to help with the pain in my jaw from biting the bullet, I fetched a wire coat hanger from my toolbox and fashioned a hook to fish through the van window and release the door catch. After all, the little scrotes that specialise in stealing vehicles can carry out this manoeuvre in seconds. Obviously, I was not cut out to be a thief, and after what seemed like hours gave up on ever gaining entry without smashing the window.

Just as I lifted the hammer to do the dirty deed, John the foreman turned the corner en route to his car, ready to leave site for the day.

'Whoa, what are you doing?' he shouted in horror at the sight of this madman wielding a hammer.

I explained what had happened regarding the lost keys, leaving out the bit about actually apportioning blame to Barry.

'Hang fire a moment. Come with me,' said John.

We returned to the site hut where the rest of the lads were

preparing to go home. Looking at one of the labourers he said, 'Hey Robert, what were you in prison for last time?'

'Stealing cars,' said Robert, nonchalantly.

John explained briefly what had happened with my situation and enquired if he would be able to assist me.

'Sure,' said Robert casually, shrugging his shoulders.

Off he went whistling, whilst we were talking, only to return approximately two minutes later.

Obviously, from the time transpired, transit vans were not his forte, and I thanked him for his efforts and said that I would have to telephone a locksmith instead.

'What the hell for? It's open,' said Robert, looking at me as though I had lost my marbles – in fact, it was only my keys that I (or someone else) had lost.

'What? You cannot be serious!' The John McEnroe impression went down like a lead balloon as he stood there smirking.

'Yeah, the passenger side door is open. No damage. Goodnight all.'

I followed him as he strolled past my van, tried the door, thanked him, and slipped him a Lady Godiva (fiver to those that do not have the knowledge of Cockney rhyming slang).

I duly climbed over the passenger seat and retrieved a roll of cable to carry on work – this was in the good old days before a bulkhead was fitted. I carried on working whilst I whistled happy in the knowledge that it was all coming together at last. In the early hours of the morning, I was relieved that I was now at a stage to go home and get a few hours sleep before starting again and duly packed up my tools. Stowing them in the passenger's side foot well, I climbed across and went to start the engine. It was at this point I realised I still had no key to start it with. I thought to myself, "Oh well, I will do as the thieves do and hot wire it" – easy enough.

I removed the covers from the ignition but then came the realisation that although I could start it by shorting out the wiring, the steering lock was engaged and needed to be disabled as well. After all, driving round in continuous circles was not going to help me get home. Once again, probably easy for some little shit that specialises in stealing other people's property but not for an honest minded electrician. A further ten minutes ensued of utilising various hammers, large screwdrivers etc, until the steering lock mechanism hung limply from the steering column. This was definitely turning into an expensive exercise, although I could now start the van and look forward to getting back home.

The van was started and off I drove on my way at last. After about five miles I glanced at the fuel gauge and realised that I would need to put in some diesel in order to get back. A few miles further down the road I pulled into a service station and went to fill up at the diesel pump, only to realise that the filler cap was locked. Guess where the key was? That is right – with all the others!

Back out came the hammer and large screwdriver again. Fighting despair, and a locked filler cap, I persevered until the filler cap disappeared into the tank. Not really what I was intending but at least I was at last able to fill up of fuel. A bin liner served as a temporary filler cap and home was at last a real possibility.

At last, the light at the other end of the tunnel was more than just a train coming the other way!

*

A time when things went drastically wrong leaps to mind – a time that would have have meant this book would not exist – or indeed I would not have existed myself!

*

On this occasion, I was working at, what at the time, was a popular

Birmingham nightclub, alongside my brother. There was a problem with the entrance lighting, and we were attempting to discover the problem and rectify it. A cable we were tracing disappeared up inside the suspended ceiling and one of us needed to access the ceiling space to find out where it led to. There is nothing like a volunteer – and I was nothing like a volunteer – but it needed doing and so the step ladder was set up and I disappeared into the void – *'Beam me up Scotty'*.

The building that now housed the nightclub had served some years previously as the pit head baths for a local colliery. The colliery had closed, the showers, baths and changing rooms removed and it now served as a venue for having meals and watching famous acts. Remember the nineteen seventies? Meals in a basket? Scampi and chips. Chicken Kiev and chips. Such exoticism that conjured up thoughts of foreign climes! The good old days eh? The soup in a basket was not such a good idea, but then not everything works (or everyone in my experience).

Anyway, up inside the suspended ceiling was a large wooden platform that served as a support base for the large, copper hot water cylinders that were once used to store the hot water for the showers. These were still in situ, probably as they were too unwieldy to remove at the time due to their vast size. The suspended ceiling served to keep all the unnecessary paraphernalia out of sight of the general public and was rarely entered.

I knelt down on the wooden platform and shouted to Brian to wiggle the cable in order that I could locate it and find out where it went. Brian did the wiggling (put it out of your minds, you awful lot! I meant the cable) whilst I found it and started following its route. It came up and over the wooden joists and then disappeared beneath the platform that I was kneeling on. I remember feeling along, to trace the route of the cable, under the timber and then suddenly everything went black!

I had apparently, inadvertently, located another cable – one that had not been isolated or made safe. I remember waking up after what only must have been a quite short period of time. I had touched the cable with my arm and must have been touching some metalwork with another part of my body, giving the electricity a course to run right through me. The resulting electric shock had made me crash my head down onto the plywood floor, causing me to be knocked out temporarily. Unfortunately, although I had now awakened, my arm was still on the cable and my neck was against one of the copper cylinders. This caused a perfect path for the electric current to keep flowing through my body. Twitching like a birdwatcher in an aviary, I was vaguely aware of what was happening to me as I lay there unable to breathe out properly but kept on breathing in spasmodically. Somehow – and to this day I still do not know how – I managed to kick against the brick wall behind me, releasing me from the continuing torture. All I had to do now was get down the steps – oh and find where the cable was running to in order to rectify the original fault (conscientious or what?). Also, I was in need of a clean pair of jeans and underpants as the ones I was wearing were very wet. Another side effect of getting electrocuted is losing control of certain vital bodily muscles and I was just glad, at this point, that I had not had a curry the night before!

It was at this point that a little head appeared through the entrance hatch. Brian had by now wondered what was taking so long and why I was not answering his attempt at communication.

I think my face was a slight giveaway as to there being something amiss, as it had split open upon impact with the platform and was now marring my Adonis like features. Also, my limp body lying sprawled out and attempting to breathe properly was a factor in him calling out to someone to call for an ambulance. I felt as though an elephant was standing on my chest and the warm wet feeling around my crotch was turning into a cold, wet smelly sensation.

As I lay there, I tried to convey what I thought had happened and the next thing I was being assisted down by two paramedics. I was placed on a stretcher, transferred to the ambulance and off we went to the hospital. Blue lights flashing and siren blaring I was taken to Sandwell hospital and rushed into accident and emergency where I was checked over and hooked up to a machine.

'What is that machine for,' I groggily asked through bloody lips.

'It is to check your heart,' replied the very nice young, blonde-haired nurse, cheerily. 'To make sure it has not done any damage and ensures it is still operating properly.'

It was at this point that I felt compelled to inform her that I did indeed not possess a heart – it had been replaced years ago by a swinging brick – or so I had been informed by my dearly beloved wife. Apparently, this was misinformation supplied to me by 'er indoors, as the machine had merrily located and was happily monitoring such an appendage.

After a couple of hours, I was collected by my father and driven home for some rest – and a change of clothes.

The next day Brian came to visit, and I asked him what had happened, and he said, 'Well, I heard a bit of a bump, followed shortly after by, "uhh, uhh, uhh, uhh" (me breathing in and in and in). I thought you had found something like a pair of dummy hands or something and was waiting for you to appear at the hatch with these hands round your neck, pretending to be being strangled. But you did not appear and was not answering me, so I decided to have a look.'

'Yeah, sounds about right,' I said. It goes to show that all that messing about on site is not always as funny as it seems – but only occasionally!

I was soon recovered and although my face took a while to heal, my good looks were eventually returned (it is my opinion and I am entitled to it), and work called me back. Thinking about it now, I never did find out what the original problem with the lights was – I can only presume Brian sorted it out at the time.

*

Another disaster that comes to mind is an occasion when I was an apprentice (thankfully). I was working with a particularly good electrician who was named Terry, at a site in Stoke-on-Trent in Staffordshire. Terry taught me a lot of good things whilst we were together but even, he was not infallible. The site belonged to a major manufacturer of ceramic tiles and was basically, at that time, no more than a large field in the middle of nowhere. For some reason, the plant was using liquid petroleum gas to run the kilns that fired the glaze on the tiles – perhaps at that time there was no mains gas available – after all this was the 1960s. The LPG was supplied by Esso and we were to carry out some work for them.

Because of the danger of fire, it was necessary to install a water sprinkler system around the enormous gas tank situated in the field. Therefore, a pump was needed to pump the water, rapidly, to the tank area and it was decided that this would be placed in the side of a small lake that was already situated on site. Because of the need for speed and quantity of water to be delivered, this pump would need to be rather on the large side.

A concrete garage had been erected, in the vicinity of the lake, prior to these works, to house the electrical switchgear that ran two small pumps near the tank. These pumps ran twenty-four hours a day in order to supply the gas up to the factory. The necessary controls for the new pump were to be installed in this existing garage.

All went well with the installation of the pump wiring and associated automatic starting equipment. All that was left was a test run to ensure that the pump did its job and delivered a volume of water almost instantaneously in the event of a fire. The pump suppliers and the pipefitters had checked their installations accordingly and the day came for lift off. We had checked and double checked the wiring etc.

Terry by-passed the automatic starting procedure and manually pressed the button to fire up the pump. The pump remained motionless, although there was an almighty bang outside the garage, directly at the point where the electricity supply was fed from an overhead pole system. This also coincided with the fluorescent light in the garage ceasing to be alight.

'Oh dear,' said Terry, 'it appears we have a problem. I think it has blown a fuse!'

Little did he know at the time that this was the understatement of the century. A few seconds later a klaxon siren, obviously sounding some sort of alarm, could be heard from somewhere in the distance. This preceded a procession of exceptionally large, expensive cars trailing down to our vicinity which proceeded to spew forth a large number of terribly angry, red-faced men in suits, some almost frothing at the mouth.

'What is going on?'

'What are you doing?'

'What the hell is happening?'

'What have you done?' were a few of the more polite questions that were bandied about all at the same time. Everyone was in a major panic – all except Terry and me that is. We just stood there blank faced until they all simmered down and stood there looking enquiringly at us.

'I think there is a problem with the new pump we were installing,' ventured Terry, as he attempted to crawl up his own arse and then drag it in after him.

'There is more than a problem with the new pump,' spat one of the suits. 'There is a problem with all the kilns being extinguished and scrapping ten thousand pounds worth of ceramic tiles!' Obviously, in that day and age, ten thousand pounds was a considerable sum of money – well in excess of two hundred thousand pounds by today's standards. I could tell somehow that he was not happy – being as intuitive as I was. For once I was only too happy to be the apprentice!

The loud bang we had heard turned out to be the electricity board's main fuses blowing adjacent to the transformer. This cut the electricity supply into the switch room and meant that the two pumps that fed the gas up to the factory had stopped also. No pumps, no gas. No gas, no flames. No flames, no heat. No heat, tiles buggered! Oops. My immense perception led me to gather why the management were not amused, as I sidled out of the garage and disappeared before the wrath of the people could found its way in my direction.

At this point I had better explain the principle of industrial type electrical wiring – please bear with me and I will try to simplify things as much as possible. When you wire a new plug top at home you have a live wire (brown), a neutral wire (blue) and an earth wire (green/yellow) – for the older generation such as I it was once, red, black and green. Everyone on board so far? Good. Now, when wiring large industrial type items, it is slightly different. There is no neutral wire. Instead, there are three live wires. These were at the time red, yellow, and blue – changed now to make life more difficult, thanks to us pulling in line with Europe. Anyway, without a very expensive instrument, which our gaffer did not bother investing in, it was impossible to tell which direction the pump motor would turn. This is not normally a problem as to reverse it all that was required was to swap any of the two live wires – 50/50 chance – and it would spin the other way. In other words, instead of the pump in question delivering water to the sprinkler system, there would have been a spectacular display of bubbles in the lake. Rather like a pod of minke whales farting, after ingesting a baked bean curry – sorry, my imagination runs riot sometimes.

What no one had happened to mention – namely the pump

manufacturers – was that in the top of this particular pump there was a large ratchet and pawl to prevent the pump running backwards. The consequence of which was the pump attempting to run contrary to requirements and being unable to do so it resulted in it blowing the fuses.

The next day there was a big meeting of all the bodies involved resulting in, I believe, Esso's insurance paying out for the damage caused and a dressing down for Terry. A lesson learned by Terry and moi – never take anything for granted.

*

Talking of taking things for granted I remember one time when I found myself working for a small but quite exclusive bathroom installation company from Birmingham. I had started out doing the electrical installation side of the projects but ended up doing whole installations from showers to full bathrooms – plumbing, electrics, tiling was all on my agenda. My talents and versatility knew no bounds in my younger years, plus I was willing to do anything for money.

On this one occasion I was installing a shower, in a bathroom, in a suburb of Birmingham. The customer wanted a recessed shower and so I was busy chiselling out the wall in the bathroom to accommodate the necessary valve and pipe work. It was a fairly ordinary three bedroomed house but decorated and dressed very tastefully.

The couple who owned the house had an exceptionally beautiful daughter – all long, blonde hair, legs up to her armpits and well built in all the right places. She also had a nice tan that was topped up frequently in the rear garden. I know this because I had seen her through the bathroom window – the small opening one that could only be accessed by standing on the side of the bath – that job was taking a long time to finish for some unknown reason. Every opportunity was taken in order to speak to her, smile at her and carefully wipe the dribble from my chin. I was sure that a date would be on the cards fairly soon as she no longer ignored me and had even started to provide tissues when talking to me, to mop up the spittle. It was only a matter of time before my wily charms overcame her formidable defences.

On this occasion the daughter must have been having a late start, as a little voice spoke daintily through the bathroom door, 'Do you really have to make so much noise? I am trying to get some beauty sleep.'

'You do not need any more beauty sleep my dear, as perfection cannot be improved on,' I countered.

What a smoothie I was. This was in the days before a smoothie became a drink of course. I did not hear the sound of retching into a bucket and consequently took this as a good sign and so I ventured, 'I am deeply sorry, but I have to conceal the shower workings and this necessitates chiselling out the wall, but I will be as quick and quiet as possible, honest.'

She sloped off back to her bed as I had visions of her negligee clad beauty lying awaiting me. After I had come to my senses, I tentatively started tapping the chisel with the hammer, afraid of upsetting her. Then again, I had a job to do and as time went on, so the hammer blows became more spirited. I knew I was safe to chisel out sufficient space for the shower as it was a breeze block wall and after all a breeze block is four inches thick is it not?

Unfortunately, not all breeze blocks are, as I was to find out very soon. Somebody somewhere had the stupid idea to manufacture two-inch-thick blocks instead, a fact that I was unaware of at the time. No doubt it was probably a material saving exercise brought about during or just after the Second World War. Happily, and ignorantly, hammering away, I suddenly felt the resistance to my blows give way to fresh air as a rather sizeable hole appeared in the wall. 'Oh shit' I cried. 'I had better have a look what has happened on the other side and see if I can fix it before anyone finds out.' Racing out of the bathroom I opened the door to the adjacent bedroom to see what damage I had caused.

There before my very eyes, was said beautiful daughter, lying in bed covered in plaster and breeze block rubble. Unable to think of anything else I blurted out 'I suppose a date is out of the question?' I immediately took her answer as a definite no. I was glad really, as a girl that can fit that many expletives into one short sentence was not a lady in my book anyway. I offered to help her clean herself up but that also went down extraordinarily badly, and I scurried away, to own up to her parents, before she had a chance to remove my testicles and force feed them down my throat in a very vicious manner as she vehemently promised.

CHAPTER 18

REVENGE – A DISH BEST SERVED COLD – VERY COLD

A tale that was related to me one day by a pair of painters I was working with could certainly stand being told here. Apparently, so the story goes, Bert and Andy, the painters in question had been asked to paint the exterior of a large house in Handsworth Wood, a suburb of Birmingham. In years gone by, Handsworth Wood had been a very affluent area and contained some very nice, large abodes. The pair had gone along, viewed and priced the job and agreed the price with the occupier. The occupier was a tall, moving mountain of a man built like the proverbial shithouse, standing about six feet, seven inches tall, covered in hair and tattoos. Despite looking as though he demolished houses with his bare hands for a living, he seemed friendly enough and the boys had been happy to carry out the work as requested.

A couple of weeks was spent rubbing down, priming, and painting all the window frames, doors, guttering etc. and it was of the general consensus that a fine job had been done indeed. These lads were very conscientious and always carried out a first-class job as far as I was aware.

*

'Right, I will clean up here,' said Bert. 'You carry on and start on that next job and I will settle up with the householder and come over to you.'

'Okay,' replied Andy, as he loaded up his van and happily disappeared up the road.

Whistling to himself, Bert finished the last vestiges of tidying away the materials and ladders, looking forward to receiving a nice wad of cash. This was always the best part of the job – being rewarded for all that hard work. Especially when the remuneration was in cold hard pound notes. No waiting for cheques to clear and not always declared as profit (allegedly).

Still whistling, Bert rang the doorbell and waited. After a couple of minutes, the man mountain opened the door, blocking out the space where it had been.

'Okay, all finished if you want to come and inspect,' said Bert.

'No, it is alright, I am sure you have done a wonderful job. I had a look round yesterday after you had left anyway, and all looked okay then.'

'Oh fine,' Said Bert. 'Then there is just the small matter of payment.'

'Yes, that could be a slight problem,' stated the man, looking grim.

'Why should that be a problem?' queried Bert.

'Well, I do not want to pay you,' said the hulk.

'What do you mean you do not want to pay me?'

'Just what I said, I do not want to pay. I get a lot of work done like that. What are you going to do about it?' he challenged.

'I will see my solicitor,' Bert stated assertively.

'Go ahead and waste your money if you wish. I do not see any written agreement or quotation, anywhere, do you?' the bear answered. 'Now move your van off my drive thank you,' he snarled aggressively.

Bert was absolutely gobsmacked that anyone could play them for such suckers and was almost tempted to head butt him in the stomach – as that was about as high as he could reach without a step ladder. Dejectedly he drove off to join Andy on the next project, hoping that a miracle would happen, and payment would be forthcoming.

Upon seeing Andy, Bert explained what had gone on, as they dejectedly started work on the next house to be done.

'What are we going to do?' asked Andy. 'We cannot just let him get away with it.'

'What can we do? It would cost a fortune to sue him and without guaranteed results and the alternative, of beating the money out of him, does not seem likely somehow. All those piercings, tattoos, hair, broken nose and scars do not look like someone I wish to fight – and that is only his wife!'

Much deliberation followed, until suddenly a light bulb came shining on, in Bert's head!

'Thank heaven for that,' said Andy. 'I hate painting in the dark.'

During the ensuing moments, a cunning plan was devised. That evening, after finishing up for the day, the lads returned to their lock up, where they kept all their materials. Over time many partly used tins of paint of every colour and hue had accumulated on the shelves. A couple of hours of careful decanting saw a variety of paints, of many different shades, loaded into polythene bags, which were then carefully sealed. These missiles were then carefully placed into a cardboard box and loaded onto the van ready for their covert mission.

Waiting until the small hours of the morning, Bert called for Andy and the boys parked just down the road from the offending property, with evil intent on their minds and fishing catapults in their pockets. Sneaking under the cover of darkness they approached the house like it was an SAS mission, armed with the box of projectiles and catapults. After careful scrutiny it was established that there were no lights on, and no one in the house appeared to be awake.

With careful aim, and following years of practise fishing, the first polythene bag of paint was launched on to the roof. This was followed by numerous others until it was felt that there was a danger of getting caught. Sneaking back to the van, giggling like two little schoolgirls, Andy and Bert left the scene, happy that retribution had been carried out.

The following morning, as soon as it was daylight, the dynamic duo decided to have a quick detour on the way to work, just to see what their handiwork looked like in the cold light of day. It turned out that it was better than expected, as a few people had stopped to view the explosion of colour that had turned the roof into a rainbow hued delight. Unable to contain themselves, the pair drove off in fits of laughter.

Later that same day Andy's phone rang, and a timid voice pleaded, 'Hi, somehow my roof has been spotted with paint of various colours. I hate to ask this but is there any way you could come and get it off for me? Please.'

'Sorry, who is this?' replied Andy, desperately trying to supress a laugh as Bert collapsed in a writhing heap on the floor.

'It is Robin, the guy who's house you finished yesterday.'

'Oh, the Robin that did not pay us for the excellent job we did?' came the sarcastically cutting retort.

'Yes, sorry about that. I was just having a bit of a lark with you. I really intended to ring you today to come and collect the money,' came the sheepish reply.

'No problem,' replied Andy. 'It will take us about one hour to get to you if we leave now, but of course that means we will get behind on this job, and therefore you would have to make it worthwhile us doing so.

'I will pay you whatever you think is realistic plus a bonus if you could get here today.'

After a quick consultation with Bert, Andy said, 'It will be one thousand pounds. Cash in the hand, of course.'

'I understand where you are coming from. I will have the money ready,' said a voice that obviously knew when he was beaten.

The lads packed up their ladders and brushes and made their way back to the nice house in Handsworth Wood. Once there they got the ladders off the van and put them up the front of the house before ringing the bell. The Neanderthal householder opened the door, ecstatic to see that the boys had been true to their word.

'Thanks a lot for coming so quickly, I really appreciate it. I may have made a few enemies along the way in life, but I know you will help me out.'

'Of course, there is just a matter of the money for the job,' said Bert.

'Cash, of course. Up front, obviously,' said Andy.

'Oh yes of course. I will fetch it whilst you make a start.'

'No, sorry, nothing gets started until we have the cash,' said Bert.

'I am afraid your track record is not squeaky clean,' said Andy.

Dejectedly, he ambled off and came back with one thousand pounds in cash. Bert counted it and then said 'Hang on a minute. What about the money for the original job? I think that ought to be forthcoming as well before we start helping you out of a hole.'

'But…'

'No buts, - no money, no job.' No likey, no lightey (borrowed that one off Paddy)! 'Sorry but you started it.'

'Okay, I suppose you have me bang to rights. You win this time around.'

Off he went again and reappeared with the original sum in cash. After counting it all the boys said in unison, 'Okay, you go off and make us a nice cup of coffee and a biscuit while we, make a start.'

Off he went to make the necessaries as requested, but by the time he reappeared with the tray there was no one to be seen. He scoured the premises before the awful truth hit home. The lads had packed up the ladders, secured them on the van and were off up the pub for a celebratory pint or two. Revenge is not only sweet but can be intoxicating as well. After a couple of days their phones stopped ringing incessantly and a message was left. Something about removing a part of their anatomies that would prevent future fatherhood and cramming them where the sun does not shine apparently. I dare say her husband was not too pleased either. Some people definitely have a distinct lack of a sense of humour! Needless to say, they did not venture up to that area again, looking for any future work.

*

Another bunch of painters, ones I worked with quite frequently, were a bunch of Irish lads. Most of them were nice enough but there was one or two of them that no one wanted to get on the wrong side of. It was generally believed that they were associated with a certain faction in Northern Ireland and indeed were 'Persona Non Grata' in England. This speculation was further fuelled by the fact they were always paid in cash, at the end of each week, despite the fact that they were more or less permanently employed contractors. A crowd of very hard-working lads, nonetheless. We were, at the time, refurbishing a large public house in south London. The time schedule for the works was very tight indeed and most of the tradesmen were putting in long hours. This, coupled with the fact that everyone seemed to be on site at the same time, led to short tempers and constant bickering. It was at times, like working with a load of old women – insults and handbags flying in all directions.

The painters like everyone else were clamouring to get the job finished. Quite often I would wonder why my legs felt so tired, only to discover a painter standing on my shoulders, painting merrily away instead of using a step ladder. The looming deadline led, almost inevitably, to short cuts being taken by some of the lads.

The project manager was a really decent fellow that I got on with particularly well. Having said that, he was extremely good at his job and had eyes like an eagle. Nothing, and I mean nothing, escaped his attention. I remember on one occasion where I had fitted hundreds of light fittings in a hotel. I had run out of brass screws and had fitted one solitary steel screw in one solitary light fitting in one obscure bathroom. It appeared on the snagging list at the end of the job to be replaced. Such was his pernicketiness (Google it, I had to)!

Anyway, he got to know about certain malpractices by the painters and went on the war path (nice man, but he did look silly wearing a feathery headdress and shaking his tomahawk). Stop it, I know what you are thinking – you smutty devils.

He requested that the foreman painter accompany him to a private room, where, judging from the ensuing arguments that were to be heard, a heated discussion took place. The foreman eventually appeared, red faced and breathing like an asthmatic dragon. This actually came in handy for burning off the paintwork that needed to be redone. The project manager appeared shortly after, composed – and minus his tomahawk, to recommence the inspection of the rest of the works.

The consequence of this altercation was that extra painters were brought onto the job and even more night work had to be carried out in order to bring the work back on to schedule.

Nothing was said by anyone for the next couple of days as tempers were a little frayed to say the least. The project manager returned a couple of days later to check on progress and parked his brand new, top of the range, cream coloured Lexus saloon car outside the premises. After about one hour, he was almost ready to leave when someone approached him and suggested that he may want to examine his car. Vacating the premise, he approached his car, only to be greeted by a very large scratch on one side, from end to end and a rather large splodge of bright red paint in the centre of the roof. To say he was not happy would be the understatement of the century.

I, along with a majority of the rest of the boys, decided that this would be a good time to go to the local café for a cup of tea and a bun. When we returned (four years later) some sense of normality had been regained and we all carried on regardless. An enquiry was carried out over the ensuing week, where we were all interviewed individually but it was never established exactly who the perpetrator was. The main contractor, who employed the painters, paid for the repairs to the car and little reference was ever made to the incident. There did though seem to be a lowering of temperature, in the vicinity, when the project manager and the foreman painter consequently came face to face after that.

*

Another incident that springs to mind was during my time as a manager at a medium sized contracting company. This was during one of the periods in my life when I worked for someone else – something I was not particularly good at. I cannot suffer fools and as it turned out the owner of this company was an arsehole of the first degree. The word arrogance was invented for this guy and let us just say that my employment with him was fairly short lived.

Although the company employed a fair number of electricians, the workload was always at such a level that a lot of agency labour was required in order to keep bodies on sites. I have worked with a lot of agency workers, and I must say that a lot of them are incredibly good, but transversely, a lot of them are in the league of leaving something to be desired. Especially if they are treated unjustly, and quite rightly so.

A job arose one day that needed someone on site the very next day and as I had no one available to call on, I had to request an

173

electrician from the labour agency. I informed the agency where the site was and arranged to meet the guy there at eight o'clock the next morning. The project was a newly built, fairly large office block just outside Birmingham. Meeting the electrician there I took him over the job, showed him the drawings and gave him the necessary cable and materials to wire the lights, sockets etc. ready for the plastering to be carried out. This would then require the second fix, where the light fittings, sockets etc. are fitted to complete the installation.

I checked on him every couple of days, or as and when my excessive workload permitted. I was flying up and down the country attempting to keep control of many and varied contracts. Boy it made my arms ache! He seemed happy enough and the job was progressing at a fair rate as the plasterers followed him along the length of the building. All was going well – or so I thought.

The boss of the company was unfortunately, not one to let a manager manage. He persistently had to interfere in matters such as labour distribution, and when no one turned up on a job, because he had sent them somewhere else, without my prior knowledge, it suddenly became my fault, and my problem to sort out. This sort of thing was carried out on a regular basis, as inevitably he knew best – or so he thought. As the office job was nearing completion of the first fix, he decided that it was not progressing quickly enough for his liking. He insisted that the agency electrician, who was doing fine, had to go that night and he would find someone else to carry on with the job. Argue as I might that it would be difficult for someone else to take over another man's job, he knew best. Out I went to deliver the bad news to the guy on site. He was not a happy bunny! Ranting and raving, he eventually packed up his tools and left the site, mad at me, despite my protestations that it was not my decision.

I suspected that the reason for the decision was to do with payments to the employment agency, as this company was infamous for late payments, often entailing being on the stop at one or more suppliers. I am surprised that he could get credit anywhere as he was quite notorious for letting his companies go bankrupt and starting up again under a different name. More than one supplier had lost big sums of money through this process. Again, it frequently turned into being my fault, if I could not procure materials, because the gaffer had not paid the bills! Marvellous.

A couple of days later I was instructed to send out one of the electricians employed direct by the company. I met him in the office and showed him the drawings and wished him the best of luck with picking up where the other lad had left off. Approximately two hours later my phone rang. It was the electrician that had been dispatched to the office block.

'I think you had better get over here pronto,' he said.

'Why, what is the problem?' I replied.

'There is no wiring in here.'

'Don't be daft, it was all but finished being first fixed. Just a few cables to be thrown across the ceilings when they are in place.'

'I am telling you, there are no cables,' he reiterated.

'I am on my way,' I stated as I picked up my attaché case (posh eh!) and left the office to cross Birmingham, as if I had nothing better to do than hold the hand of somebody who obviously either needed a lesson in cable identification or should have gone to Specsavers. (Any commission can be forwarded through my agent.)

Upon eventually arriving on site, I sought the electrician, only to be reliably informed that he had been called off to another site. Number one 'arsehole' had struck again.

Now, beyond despair, I went off to examine the missing wiring that I knew was there, because I had seen it. With my own eyes indeed – this was no figment of my imagination. But no matter where I looked, sure enough there was no sign of any cables, save for a few noticeably short pieces protruding from the metal boxes that were recessed into the walls. Fearing now for my own sanity I examined the installation closer. Upon close scrutiny it became apparent that every single visible piece of cable had been cut off where the plaster line finished – a nice, neat job indeed! We have a problem Houston!

I returned to the office, where *'the anal orifice'* had, by now gained the knowledge that something was amiss. Summoned straight to his office I was quizzed over the problem that was apparently, lo and behold, my fault.

'Hold on a moment,' I said, 'how do you conclude that it was my fault?'

'Well, it is quite obvious who carried out the dastardly deed,' came the sneering reply.

'And would you care to enlighten me as to the character that has appeared in your crystal ball?' I scorned.

'Obviously, it was the agency guy that you sacked. He was seeking some form of retribution.'

'Well, that could be true. But just as easily it could have been anyone that fancied stealing the cables, for the copper content. After all there is no security on site outside of normal working hours and the price of copper scrap is high at this moment in time.' Why I was defending the obviously guilty party I am not too sure, but I had an inkling of what was about to emanate.

'No, it must have been that tosser. He knew exactly what was what,' came the reply.

'Well, we can speculate all day long, but it would take some proving as to who the culprit really was,' I disputed.

Then he countered with an absolute masterpiece. 'I am sure of whom it was, and I hold you responsible.'

I could not believe my ears and reminded him that it was him that had insisted that the guy's services were dispensed with.

'Well, there are ways of getting rid of people without upsetting them,' he volunteered. 'This is going to cost an absolute fortune to put right. You had better organise a team of electricians to get it sorted as soon as possible and I want it done with no additional expense to the company.'

'And how do you propose I do that? Tell all the guys that they will be working for nothing?' I said as steam started to emanate from my ears. 'This cock up is not of my making.'

'I do not care how you do it but if you wish to keep your job you will organise it,' he said pulling himself up to his full five feet two inches.

The red mist descended as I looked him square in the eyes and sweetly said, 'You know what, you can stick your job firmly where the sun does not shine, you arrogant son of a bitch.At that I turned away and walked out of his office, slamming the door on the way out. I walked to my desk and was in the throes of emptying it when he appeared by my side.

'Perhaps I was a little hasty there. Let us forget what was said and set about putting the job right eh?' He knew that it would take considerable organising and boot licking and obviously did not want to be saddled with it himself.

I looked him up and down and vehemently stated between gritted teeth, 'I would rather stick pins in my eyes than work for some jumped up little shit like you for a minute longer.' The whole office gasped in unison. Actually, it was in Birmingham, but it is my book, and I can write it how I like. Accidentally leaving the company car's keys in my pocket, I left and never went back. I eventually got the wages that were owing to me paid into the bank, after which they got the keys to the car back. It disappeared from my drive a couple of days later and nothing more was heard from the company. Like I said, I was not really cut out to work for others.

I did hear on the grapevine shortly after that the company had gone into liquidation – again – leaving many suppliers and sub-contractors out of pocket – again!

*

Whilst working in another public house, in London, an opportunity to bring another arrogant sole to earth was presented to me on a platter.

The job was almost complete after many weeks of hard work. It is always a great feeling to see the fruits of your labour come to fruition. It also often meant free food and free beer as the staff training would take place at this time and we were usually the guinea pigs – very willing ones indeed.

All that remained to be done was the finishing touches. This included the pictures being hung and the bric-a-brac being placed on the shelves. The place was almost pristine, and the cleaners were scheduled for that afternoon to complete the job ready for the grand opening that night.

Most of the men had left site by this stage, just a skeleton staff of workers (perhaps I should not speak of skeletons, given what had transpired here previously – see chapter one) ready to clean up and finish off. The only others on site were the project manager and his quantity surveyor, checking that everything had been carried out to the satisfaction of their client. Their presence was supplemented from time to time by various members of the brewery hierarchy popping in to keep an eye on the latest flagship to their portfolio.

In walked the bric-a-brac men, bringing with them all the pictures and associated items for the displays. The project manager greeted them and gave them their instructions and then left them to their own devices. Almost immediately the leader of their team walked across and picked up a knife from out of a toolbox that was situated on the floor. My toolbox! No please, or thank-you, just helped himself and turned to carry on.

'Whoa, just a minute mate,' I said casually. 'What do you think you are doing?'

'Just borrowing a knife,' he replied arrogantly. 'What's your problem?'

'My problem is that is my toolbox, and that is my knife, and I do not appreciate strangers swanning in here and removing items without my permission.'

'It's only a knife!' His Cockney accent was by now starting to grate on my nerves.

'Yes, my knife, not yours,' I replied.

'I was going to put it back when I had finished. No need to get arsey. I just wanted to open some of the wrappings on our stuff.'

'That is fine, but you ask before you borrow my tools, okay? I do not know you from Adam.'

'Please sir, may I borrow your knife for a few minutes?' he said in his most sarcastic, childish voice. 'And by the way, my name is Adam.'

'Well Adam, yes you may borrow my knife but please be careful as it is very sharp. I would hate you to cut a vital artery or something,' I replied acrimoniously. 'After all the place is opening soon and it would not look good with blood splattered up the walls.'

It was plain to see that we were never going to become bosom buddies as he huffed his way across the floor. We both returned to our tasks and nothing more was said – until about thirty minutes later. Everything was taking great shape until there was a large bang followed by a number of the lights going out. Fortunately, on the one hand, this proved that the emergency lighting was operating correctly. On the other hand, this was not what was supposed to happen at this stage. My immediate thoughts were that some part of our installation had malfunctioned just at a critical time. I was just ready to disappear from view when I spied Adam staggering around, momentarily blinded and wondering what had happened. He was holding a cordless drill with a drill bit that looked slightly melted at the end, rather like a smoking gun. Obviously, he had drilled somewhere that he should not have done.

'What have you done?' I shouted, noticing a small wisp of smoke emanating from a hole in the wall near to where Adam was standing, looking very sheepish and red faced – the first red faced sheep I have ever seen incidentally. It was becoming quite obvious what had happened, as a satisfied smirk crept up my face.

The project manager plus his surveyor and two brewery employees made their way in the general direction of the furore. By this time Adam had recovered and said very meekly, 'I was just drilling a hole to hang a picture when there was a loud bang, and I was thrown backwards.'

'You have obviously drilled through a cable,' I said. Stating the obvious has always been one of my stronger points.

'Well, what a stupid place to have a cable,' pleaded Adam defensively.

'What, right below a wall light fitting?' interjected the project manager.

The small black hole in the wall was approximately one hundred millimetres (that is four inches in old money, for the dinosaurs amongst you) below a wall light and directly in line with it. That particular light had been wired from below, through necessity, as had others as it was not possible in some instances to access above the ornate ceiling.

'How was I to know there was a cable there? Normally the cable comes down the wall,' Adam pleaded.

"The light fitting just above should have been a slight clue,' stated the project manager. 'Did you check with a detector before you drilled?'

'No, unfortunately I forgot to bring it with me,' mumbled a little voice.

'It is probably with your knife,' I volunteered. Childish I know given the circumstances, but I was unable to forego the opportunity that was handed to me on a silver salver.

The project manager looked at me and pleadingly said, 'Can you repair it alright?'

'I can but it is not going to be easy. Or cheap,' I replied. 'I am going to have to fetch up part of the new carpet and the floorboards below that and see if I can drag a new cable through. It is not going to be a five-minute job.'

'Do your best. I will cover whatever costs you incur,' stated the project manager who then turned around to Adam and said, 'I will stop the cost of whatever Alan charges from your invoice. Plus, any other work that is needed to repair the wall.'

My nose twitched as that all too familiar smell of retribution (and money) wafted in my nostrils. I could envisage the blank cheque being placed in my grubby little paw as I gave Adam my best smile. I nearly said, *'Keep the knife, I will be able to afford a new one,'* but my conscience would not allow it. That, and the fact that everyone including the brewery men were all still in earshot.

That was the easy part. The hard part was actually repairing the problem. I found that one of the electricity board's main incoming fuses had blown. These fuses were fitted with anti tamper seals to prevent anyone accessing them and availing themselves of free electricity. I informed the project manager of this latest twist of events, who told me that he would ring the electricity board and explain the problem.

'That is all well and good,' I explained 'but they will probably take a few hours to get here. Obviously, that is time we do not have as the place is due to open in a couple of hours.

'Is there anything you can do?' he pleaded.

'Well,' I replied. The smell of filthy lucre arose once again to sweeten the air around me. 'I think I may have a replacement fuse I can use, but I could get into big trouble if the electricity board finds out I have broken their seal.' Laying it on thick and making it sound like a fairly hopeless task was sure to increase the remuneration.

'I will ensure that it is worth your while taking the risk,' said the project manager. 'I will also put in a good word with the suits indoors – there are a few good refurbishments in the pipeline.' I had never before really got to refurbish a pipeline – probably as I am too tall to fit in – but was always willing to try and make more money.

RIGHT ANSWER!

Fortunately, the seals in those days were of the old lead sort. These days they are made of titanium or some such sort of material that is totally tamperproof. With a little assistance from a nine-volt PP3 battery and a bit of jiggery pokery, the fuse was replaced along with the lead seal, and no one was any the wiser, that anything had happened, except my future bank account.

Whilst I lifted the carpet and the floorboards to access the cable, the decorator was rooting around in the skip for a suitable section of wallpaper to patch up with. He was still acting as a skip rat as the driver hooked up the skip to remove it from site, in order to find an offcut that would hide the black hole caused by Adam.

Meanwhile I spliced in a section of cable and pulled it up on the old, damaged cable to affect a repair. It was only a couple of hours to the official opening and the building was starting to buzz with various dignitaries from the brewery and the companies that had carried out the refurbishment. They were all standing around looking important and wondering when we would have some lighting whilst I beavered

MY PLUG IN YOUR SOCKET

away at my task. Occasionally one of them would saunter over and enquire as to when normal service would be resumed. I constantly assured them that I was doing my utmost and that I would be finished soon, demonstrably wiping the sweat from my brow for effect.

I replaced the defective cable and tentatively switched-on row after row of lights. There was a general sound of applause and congratulatory noises as the time rapidly approached to open the doors. Indeed, I was still re-fitting the carpet as the doors opened to greet the horde of enthusiastic revellers outside – it is amazing what the promise of free drinks can attain.

I put away my tools in the van and made my way back inside where I was periodically plied with alcoholic beverages from men in suits, assuring me that my actions had been noted and that it would not be forgotten. I was already envisaging the private yacht and Lear jet (I could dream once upon a time) that would soon be on order.

Needless to say, I was suitably remunerated for my rescue mission – Indiana Jones (no relation as far as I know) eat your heart out.

*

I mentioned in chapter 10 a certain plumber that never paid me the money that he owed me. He must have made more enemies than me, and someone, somewhere, certainly ensured that he got his comeuppance.

I heard the story through a wholesale supplier and therefore cannot definitely state that all the facts and figures were fully accurate, but I believe it to be so.

This particular plumber did a lot of private jobs, for cash, and pocketed the money without informing the Inland Revenue. Not a unique situation I hear you say, as many self-employed people did the same, and probably still do so – but some people do get greedy. And greedy people tend to be the ones that get caught.

In this instance, someone with a grievance against him made an anonymous telephone call to the Inland Revenue. I wish to verify at this point that it definitely was not me. I was not so creative or vindictive, although I do admit to having had a little snigger when I heard the story. It was alleged that X had been carrying out cash paid work and not declaring it. The authorities just love a lead like this and are quick to act upon such information. This was in the days when the Inland Revenue and the VAT (under the guise of customs) were separate bodies, not under one umbrella as nowadays.

One evening, shortly after the call, X received a ring on the front doorbell of his nice bungalow in the countryside. His wife answered the door to find two rather officious looking gentlemen standing there displaying their identity passes. One was from the Inland Revenue, the other from the VAT office. For anyone that is not aware, the VAT officials had more power of entry into residential premises than even the police – they did not need a warrant. Brushing X's wife aside, they swept into the lounge, where he was sat with his feet up, cradling a bottle of beer and watching television.

They explained where they were from and that they were reliably informed that he had been less than forthcoming with information regarding payment of the required taxes. The next two hours were spent gathering up any and every scrap of information that could possibly be of assistance. They confiscated his computer (more of a word processor in those days), files of paperwork, ledgers etc. and even carbon paper from the bin in his office. All this was removed from the premises along with his van containing his tools and materials required for jobs pending.

Apparently, the two offenders spent the night worrying themselves sick as to how much would be uncovered and what the consequences would be. A telephone call to his accountant early the next morning put the wheels into motion and after a couple of days pleading the van was released. After all, as the accountant argued, how could X earn any money, to repay any outstanding sum, if he could not work?

The accountant took over the negotiations with the authorities which were drawn out over a few weeks. It was touch and go as to whether a custodial sentence would be forthcoming and again it was only the reasoning that he would be unable to repay any sums if he were squandering his time at Her Majesty's service that won the day. Allegedly, various sums were bandied back and forth between the accountant and the officialdom but eventually it was conceded that they would settle for a repayment of seventy-five thousand pounds over a period of five years. At the time that represented working extremely hard, for no visible return, for a period of at least three years, possibly longer.

An awfully expensive lesson learned and a warning to many others – who shall remain anonymous.

*

At a pub refurbishment in Bristol that I did there was a large commercial kitchen to be fitted. The building itself was around six-hundred years old, a lovely timber framed, very large establishment on the dockside. As it was such a large building, it was to house a large restaurant, apart from the number of bars, also offering nourishment, and a function room. Therefore, the kitchen was to be larger than would normally be required, in order to cope with numerous culinary delights.

A vast majority of the equipment contained in such an area has to have an electrical supply and working to the supplied drawings I grafted extremely hard to wire in all the points required. As this phase of the work came to a close, I stood back and admired my handiwork – all the cables suitably covered, leading to all the metal boxes ready to terminate into the relevant switchgear. I always took a pride in my work and was especially in awe of this particular area, containing so many accoutrements. I had even ensured that I had tucked in all the cables into the boxes where possible in order to make life easier for the plasterers. I walked away from site feeling elated that next time I returned, the plastering would have been carried out and it would be ready for me to fit out all the switches, sockets etc.

I carried on with other projects in between, waiting for the plasterers to finish.

Ten days later I arrived back on site, laden down with all the equipment with which to kit out the kitchen. I was really looking forward to getting it ready for the kitchen appliances that would be arriving later that week. I could then connect the aforementioned apparatus and look forward to savouring the chef's cuisine. Making my way up to the first floor, ready to do battle, I walked into the relevant area to be greeted by an amazing site. Acres of drying pink plaster, smooth as a baby's bum. No sign of any electrical boxes or cables – just acres of drying pink plaster, smooth as a baby's bum. The plasterer had made an excellent job – except for one small detail – he had plastered straight over the boxes.

We have a problem Houston (again). Although I still had the drawings showing the approximate positions of the equipment, the actual position of the switchgear was left to me to decide and was not a fixed science. Without being able to see them, I knew roughly where they were, but not the exact positions.

I found the foreman and explained what had happened, who in turn phoned the project manager. The project manager rang me for an accurate explanation. He assured me that he would ring the plasterer and demand that he attended site the next day in order to patch up any damage that I may have to inflict.

I set to work, confident that I knew the location of most of the boxes. Oh, how the mind can play tricks when faced with a blank canvas. Hammer marks were everywhere across the walls by the time I had located them all. At high level, low level and in between it resembled something like a wall from the battle of the Somme. I was not being vindictive at all, but when face with one solid wall of plaster it is almost impossible to locate the needed positions at first try.

The following morning, I was working away when the plasterer approached, whistling like a canary on steroids. Until he saw his former pride and joy that was. I thought he was going to have an apoplectic fit as his whistling came to an abrupt halt and his bottom lip nearly hit the floor. Shouting profanities and threatening physical damage to anyone in the vicinity, I took the opportunity to go up the road and avail myself of a hearty breakfast. On the way out of the building I told the foreman that he was needed urgently in the new kitchen.

On my return from breakfast, I was greeted by a surly face that resembled a chewed wine gum. He was not happy to say the least, but I knew I was in the right, and reminded him that next time he may just want to consider the other professions on site. No one wants to do a job twice but if it is done right the first time it alleviates a costly return. He did not get paid to put his mistake right and indeed had to stand an invoice from me, via the project manager, for wasted time.

The moral of the story – Do not mess with the sparkies – especially when the project manager is a personal friend of his.

CHAPTER 19

APPRENTICESHIP –

A BLESSING OR A CURSE?

An apprenticeship for a trade is a truly marvellous thing. Perhaps if today's youngsters were less obsessed with university (or appearing on television, being an idiot, and becoming famous for nothing, to make easy money) and more interested in doing a good day's work the world would be a better place. Do not get me wrong, I know that we need academics but not everyone is cut out for that sort of life. Taking up a proper trade – such as an electrician (not things like plumbing) will ensure work for the rest of your life if the right dedication is applied. I suppose the same could be broadly said for plumbing but there is a lifelong rivalry on site between electricians and plumbers. I once considered being a plumber, but my dad said to take up a real trade and anyway I could not afford the lobotomy.

Learning a trade is never easy but can be fun, although like every part of life it can have its drawbacks. Any mistakes made by the tradesman you are working with, you cannot be blamed for, such as a pump trying to run the wrong direction – chapter 17. Alternatively, being stuck on the top of a twenty-five-foot-high aluminium scaffolding tower, crapping your pants, whilst your so-called mates are on the ground, firing blobs of glazing putty out of copper tubes at you is slightly off-putting (I am sure I still bear the bruises). This was surely the forerunner of paintballing, as the final outcome in the form of bruising is pretty much the same. But that is all part of the initiation rights that one is likely to be subjected to. Believe me there are much worse things.

In this PC world that we now reside in, it would no doubt be tantamount to bullying but I am afraid that it is part of life and will not cease no matter how many do-gooders think otherwise. The first time that I was instructed to hold the leads of an electrical tester, so that the electrician I was working with could test it, resulted in me getting an electric shock. Yes, it hurt, but I did not go running to the management crying about cruelty and being picked on. Instead, I cast aspersions on his parent's marital status and looked forward to trying it out on someone else when I was an electrician. If you cannot stand a bit of joking and banter, then an apprenticeship is not for you – go off and be an idiot on television instead. The ones that are man enough (or woman enough) can get the job done and then go forth into the wide world and make some good honest money.

Anyway, rant over, back to the stories.

*

A case in point comes to mind where some work was carried out at Winson Green prison in Birmingham. The two electricians and two apprentices had been there for a couple of weeks carrying out some lighting upgrade work. They were constantly accompanied by at least one warder and at most times two. This was to ensure that no harm came to them, from the inmates, and also to ensure that they did not supply the prisoners with anything, either deliberately, or by the belief, of certain of the residents, that if it is not screwed down or locked up, it belongs to me. Friendly banter usually ensued on a daily basis between the tradesmen and the convicts. Apart from being an experience for the working lads, it helped to while away the time for the other guys who, on the whole, were usually friendly enough.

The job was progressing very nicely when one of the apprentices had to take a couple of weeks off for a holiday that had been previously planned. This was not a problem as there was always a pool of apprentices from which to pick a replacement. It was decided that Nicholas would be enlisted for the ongoing duration of the project. Nicholas, or Nick as he was referred to, quite appropriately in this instance (think about it), was a very timid, quiet, unassuming lad. He worked extremely hard and would undoubtedly one day become a good spark, but it was difficult to elicit an in-depth conversation from him. In fact, he would not say *'boo to a goose'*. Quite why anyone would want to say *'boo'* to a goose is quite beyond my comprehension but there you are. It is a free country (allegedly), and you can do as you wish as long as it is legal.

He was informed of the decision and the following Monday morning he was waiting in the workshop, boots blacked and ready to go to prison. On the journey there the other three attempted to draw him into conversation to no avail and as there were no geese about anyway the trip was quite uneventful. He was informed of what the job entailed and what was expected of him. He was also warned about wandering off on his own as danger lurked around every corner in prisons.

'The place is full of rapists and murderers,' said one of the electricians to Nick. 'Also, a lot of them are queer (in those days gay only meant happy) as they are incarcerated 24-hours a day without any sign of women. A virgin such as yourself would be a great prize to many of those lads.'

Nick just sat there, silently staring into space, contemplating what he had been volunteered for. Upon arrival the normal work practices were commenced and the job progressed. Around mid morning all was going well, as Nick stood there at the top of a large step ladder, connecting light fittings, as instructed. He was in a world of his own, happily doing the job that he had come to love. He suddenly noticed that everything seemed to have gone very quiet and glanced down to see what was going on. To his horror, all his workmates had disappeared, along with the warders. All that he could see was a bunch of prisoners leering up at him.

'Hey, see you sonny, hurry up and finish that job. I would like to show you my cell, I bet you have not seen one before,' a broad Glaswegian accent said.

'Get away Jock, he's mine,' said a Geordie lilt.

'I doe think so Mucka,' came a black country voice. 'I ay sin a fresh 'un around here for yonks.'

Nick sat there petrified, wondering where the warders were, along with his colleagues. The voices below carried on their requests which became more intimate and disgusting as the minutes ticked by. Nick became more and more agitated, imagining it was now only a matter of seconds before he was dragged, kicking and screaming, into a cell where numerous thugs would have their wicked way with his body.

As Nick was just about to burst into tears, a voice appeared from nowhere saying, 'Okay lads that is enough now. Leave him alone and get on with your recreation.' One by one the prisoners drifted away until Nick was left alone on top of the steps shaking like a leaf in the wind, unable to believe he had been spared a fate worse than death. Around the corner came the lads accompanied by the warders, all doubled up with laughter at the sight of the quivering lump of jelly atop the step ladder.

'Come on down Nick, I think you may be in need of a strong cup of tea and a bacon sandwich,' said one of the lads.

Nick descended the steps faster than a rat up a drainpipe, still shaking and angry at his own naivety. He realised that he had been set up and looked around at everyone, who were still in raptures.

'Your face was an absolute picture,' ventured a voice, which was barely able to speak due to laughter.

'You had better keep this handy in your pocket, just in case,' was also ventured, as he was handed a tube of KY Jelly.

Nick suddenly found his voice, as he berated all around him with a verbal tirade of language that shocked even the time hardened inmates. Words were bandied about that few people, if any, had encountered before.

Later, after work, Nick was taken to a local hostelry and treated to a few pints of Mitchell and Butler's best for his troubles and thereafter was just one of the lads. Perhaps a cruel way to be brought out of his shell, but it had the desired effect, as he became not just a good electrician but a cherished member of the team. Sometimes it just takes a little shove in the right direction for someone to become their hidden inner self.

*

The establishment where I learned my trade, as an apprentice electrician, was a very well known and respected contracting company in Birmingham. The opportunities to learn were very good as the broad variety of contracts undertaken were many and varied. Two of the down sides of the company were their willingness to send apprentices out on their own to carry out jobs, and to terminate their employment as they approached their twenty-first birthday. These things were money making/saving exercises designed to benefit the company – send out a youngster to do the job and charge the full rate of an electrician and then give him his cards before he is entitled to a full wage packet. Both of these things happened to me. I was quite frequently sent out on jobs from the age of eighteen and then I was relieved of my employment a week before my twenty-first birthday.

Fortunately, I took the opportunity of working alone as a chance to learn quicker. Faced with an enigma, I muddled my way through until I knew how to do the job. This stood me in good stead for later years and I have never turned down work because I did not have any knowledge of that particular project. A little thought always overcame any doubts.

*

One windy, wet, snowy night in the depths of winter, I received a phone call from one of the directors of the company asking if I could do a small job for him. I was only eighteen at the time but more than capable of working alone – as demonstrated by the company. I reluctantly agreed, not knowing what he had in store, and duly met him thirty minutes later, on the forecourt of a petrol service station in Birmingham.

I had already explained to him that my tools were still on site and that I was limited as to what I would be able to achieve. He, in turn, explained that he had rung around the usual electricians that were in his employment but was unable to get anyone else out and how thankful he was for my services. Apparently, the problem was all the lights and signage at the front of the garage had failed and it looked as though the establishment was closed. Obviously, this was costing them money in lost business, and they were very keen to get back to normal.

I looked around the site and eventually traced the problem to a cable that had blown up in a manhole in the centre of the forecourt. That was the easy part. Not only did we have very few tools between us, but this was a special type of cable that had to be kept perfectly dry whilst being terminated. Very difficult under the circumstances as by now it was snowing quite heavily. Nevertheless, I persevered utilising my coat as a shelter and attempted a repair job. This particular type of cable needs a specific set of tools and termination equipment, neither of which I had, but with a little determination and a lot of luck I attempted and overcame the task in hand. By the time I had stripped the original termination and re-utilised it, I was frozen and sodden but had somehow managed to affect a repair of sorts. I was not entirely sure that it would not blow up again and it was indeed with some trepidation that I switched on. Success – on this occasion anyway. Brownie points were earned alongside a bonus in the pay packet.

Things did not always work out so well, as can be ascertained below.

*

On another occasion I was sent to a garage on the edge of a small village in deepest North Wales. The sort of outback, not too far from Rhyl actually, where the men are men – and the sheep live in trepidation (no that is not the name of the village).

The distribution board (commonly known as a fuse board to the non-technical) needed changing for the latest up to date version. A fairly straightforward enough job for a qualified electrician – or an apprentice. Or so you would think.

Easy enough – isolate the electricity supply by removing the main fuse, remove the old board, fit the new one, reconnect and bingo, job's a good 'un.

I explained the procedure to the person in charge and pointed out that they would have to close for a couple of hours as there would not be anything working except me.

'Okay,' said the man cheerily. Here are the keys, I might as well pop-up home for a cuppa, the wife is off work today.' Winking, he tossed a bunch of keys across to me.

Off he disappeared, in a flash, leaving me to it. It is always better to be left to get on with the job in hand, rather than having someone breathing down your neck waiting for you to finish. After all, that is when something usually goes wrong and makes you look like an idiot.

Okay, first job, locate the incoming electricity board supply and isolate the supply. Obviously, this was in the small brick built shed, adjacent to the side of the kiosk, where the distribution board is located. Just a case of finding the right key and away we go. After ten minutes of meticulously trying every key on the bunch that 'Taffy' left, it transpired that there was not one that fitted. I did not see even in which direction he had walked, not that I would have known where he lived even if I had.

Back to the drawing board, I thought to myself. I looked again at the job in hand and realised that I would have to do it without turning off the electrickery. Easy enough, as long as I was careful. Just loosen off the screws on the main incoming live cable, ease it out of the terminal and apply some insulation tape and the rest is easy. So, I loosened off the screws and secured the cable in a pair of well insulated pliers. A small bit of pressure soon made me realise that it had not been disturbed in a long time but a bit more force would surely see it eased out. Maybe a bit more then. Going purple in the face gave me an inkling that this job may not be so easy as I first thought but persistence will surely win the day.

More and more power was applied and a little wiggle given to coerce the little devil out but just as I was about to give up it seemed to move a little. 'Got you, you little blighter' or words to that effect were uttered, as in almost slow motion, the cable yielded, flew out of the connection and amidst a blinding flash of light and a very loud bang, touched down on the metal casing.

Picking myself up off the floor, I rubbed my eyes and stood there bewildered as my swimming vision started to return and my shaking hands returned to something pertaining to normality. Boy, was I glad that 'Taffy' had opted for a cuppa – or whatever he was up to. Usually there is always someone around to witness you making an almighty goof.

This action had obviously removed the immediate danger of electrocution to me by isolating the supply. This was undoubtedly due to the fact that the fuse on the incoming supply had blown and would need replacing. Like any decent (clumsy) electrician, I carried one or two replacement spares in my toolbox. This would have to wait for 'Taffy' to return and point out the missing key but would not present a problem in the ensuing period.

Carefully checking that there was indeed no electricity on the cable coming into the premises, I recommenced the job in hand and changed the necessary board. I was feeling rather proud of myself by the time 'Taffy' returned, having just completed the task that I had been set.

When he returned, his face was a mixture of elation and sadness. He went on to explain that he had taken the opportunity of a trip homeward to treat his wife to an unexpected frolic between the sheets (too much information, thank you). Apparently, they had only been married a short time and were still enjoying the practise for making babies. For us older, and longer married men it is called 'memories'.

As much as this had put a spring in his step, he did not seem to be entirely happy.

'Well considering you have just enjoyed your nuptials; you do not seem to be whistling 'Hen Wlad Fy Nhadau' (look it up!) and grinning like the proverbial Cheshire cat. What went wrong?' I asked, not really wanting an answer, but politely making conversation.

'Well, you know what it is like, isn't it? (Welsh accent required again). Supposedly, the three best things in life are a pint before and a fag after. Well, I am not bothered about the pint before, but I do prefer a fag and a nice cup of tea after, you see. Well, I came to put the kettle on and realised after a while that it was not working. I checked everything but there was nothing working at all. I called round at the neighbour's house and then at the corner shop, but it seems as if the whole village has lost all electricity. Do you have any idea what could have happened?'

'Me? No, no idea at all, although if there is a fault in the local sub-station that could account for it. Have you notified the electricity board?' I sheepishly replied – and then immediately realised that this part of the universe was no place to be acting sheepish.

'Yes, I and a few others have telephoned the electricity company and they are looking into it,' he replied.

'Well, I am sure they will fix it soon. Incidentally, I could not find the key to that small adjacent outbuilding. Could you show me which one it is please?' I enquired.

'Oh, that is not locked, you just need to prise it open with a screwdriver, the door has swollen with the damp. Did you need it open to do the job?'

'No not at all, it would just have made life a little easier.' I lied through clenched teeth. 'I will have to hang on and make sure everything is working alright when the power returns, so I will just have a mooch in the cupboard while I am waiting.'

Sure enough, with a slight bit of pressure, the cupboard door flew open to reveal the incoming main cable along with the main fuse. Ironically, there was not even a seal on the fuse and so it was an easy matter to check to see if it had blown. It was still intact. The surge had obviously been of such magnitude that it had bypassed that fuse and gone back to the sub-station, where it had treated the whole village to a blackout.

I sat and chatted to 'Taffy', unable to go home until I was sure that everything was in working order, unable to even have a cup of tea. After what seemed hours, but was in actual fact around an hour, we spotted the local electricity board's van hurtling up the road, shortly followed by the return of the power. After ensuring all was working, I wished farewell to 'Taffy' and put as much distance between myself and that place as possible before someone figured out what had transpired. A costly lesson quickly learned indeed.

*

Whilst I was an apprentice in the nineteen seventies, I was sent, along with another apprentice named Trevor and two qualified electricians Colin and Arthur, to wire up a large paper warehouse, just outside Newcastle on Tyne. No, the warehouse was not made of paper, it was to store paper, bloody big rolls of it. I have no idea what the northeast of England is like nowadays but in those far-off days it was like paradise to a seventeen-year-old lad. Loads of single girls, relatively few men and good beer. What more could a boy want? If I had died and gone to heaven, I imagined at the time that it would have been similar.

This was my first major contract as an apprentice, and my first time working away from home and so I fully intended to spread my wings and enjoy myself, along with Trevor, the other *Jack the lad*' apprentice. Upon entering the site, we dutifully reported to the foreman's hut.

Upon hearing our accents, the foreman asked, 'Where are you boys from?'

'Birmingham,' we all answered in unison.

'Watch the beer!' came the unsolicited advice. 'You will never drink more than six bottles of Newcastle Brown!' This was the days when it was only available in bottles and was extremely strong - as we were soon to find out.

By this time Trevor is rolling around on the floor in raptures of mirth. Ten or twelve pints of Ansells mild ale in a night was the norm for him and indeed he was capable of downing five or six in a lunch hour. As it happened, he and I actually drank six bottles each one night plus we shared a bottle between us on the bus back to the digs. That was the night that we were sat on the garden wall of a house, having difficulty finding our lodgings, with one 'Geordie' policeman threatening to find us accommodation for the night if we did not make ourselves scarce. By gad that was some powerful potion!

The job started out as it should – we worked hard during the day, and we partied hard at night. It even reached the stage where sometimes we would stay in at night and play cards rather than go out drinking and on the pull. After all the money we were getting was good, as we were putting in the hours, but seven days is sometimes a long time. In fact, drinking hard and having your wicked way with grateful women for fourteen days can make you too weak. Think about it! Sometimes the landlady's husband would ask if he could play cards with us, and I think it was this that led to us getting politely booted out as he sometimes ended up losing more in a night than we were paying for accommodation in a week.

Even going to the pub every lunch time became too much and so we took to passing our breaks with other pastimes. Necessity being the mother of invention (I never found out who the father was) a cricket bat was fashioned out of a piece of wood and a ball, created from a core of some unknown substance, and copious amounts of insulation tape. This occupied many of our breaks until there came a break too many – Colin's leg. Running to catch the ball he inadvertently stepped over a ridge, in the concrete floor, inside the warehouse and suffered what was obviously a nasty fracture. Arthur ran him to the hospital where his left leg was plastered up to the knee. Unlike Trevor and I who went to the pub and got plastered up to, and above, our necks. Obviously, two apprentices could not carry on working without the supervision of their superiors. Later that day we waved him off as he started the long drive back to Birmingham, slightly handicapped by a rather heavy foot on the clutch. Very inconvenient for the rest of us as we had to suffer public transport for a few days whilst a replacement electrician was procured and dispatched. The version of events given to the management was obviously vastly different. Indeed, the story went something like Colin being a hero for tripping whilst carrying materials across the site.

CHAPTER 20

MISCELLANEOUS – OTHERWISE KNOWN AS OTHER STUFF THAT I HAVE SINCE REMEMBERED

This chapter is made up of other incidents that I recall, and either do not fit into previous chapters, or alternatively I could not be arsed to go back and put them in. As I said before it is my book, and I can do it as I please. They are not in any particular order, just as I think of them or as they are in my notes.

*

It comes to mind about some of the properties I was unfortunate to happen across on my journeys. The way some people live really is beyond my comprehension, whether by choice or circumstance or not having (in their minds) a choice.

Life is a constant string of choices and each of us has to decide what choice to make (the philosophy is included in the price of the book).

One of the newsagent properties in Birmingham I attended had the living accommodation at the rear of the shop. One went through the shop and the stock room and down to the lounge and kitchen and up to the bedrooms. It was an unusual construction, being built on the side of a hill. One time, some of us were instructed to go to the property as the management of the shop had done a moonlight flit the previous night and taken the keys to the shop with them.

I turned up at the same time as the carpenter who effected entry into the shop and proceeded to change the locks. The staff member that worked in the shop and had been waiting to enter, was requested to carry on serving customers as well as possible under the circumstances, assisted by the regional manager that turned up soon after. No one could open the till and there was no small change to use, but business had to go on as normal as possible.

The carpenter was also a general all-round maintenance man and did many of the jobs needed, with the exception of the electrical and plumbing work. He asked me to go and check on the electrics in the living accommodation to see if anything needed renewing/replacing, as no one, except the previous manager and his family had been allowed into the living quarters for some time. Indeed, as it transpired, no member of staff was even allowed into the stock room. All replacement stock was fetched by the manager or his wife.

After he had gained access into the rear door, I went upstairs first. There was a definite aroma to the premises that was quite unpleasant, but this was not unusual. Often the living quarters were treated with disdain by the people running the shops.

Looking in the bedrooms and bathroom upstairs, it appeared that no one had set foot into these rooms for quite some time. All the lights were working, and the rest of the electrical equipment seemed to be in order. So far, so good.

My next port of call was down the other stairs. As no keys were available for this door either, entry was once more effected by the carpenter. As soon as the door was opened, the stench attacked the noses of us unfortunate enough to be in range. As I stated, many of the premises were rough, but not to this extent. I instructed the carpenter, who I shall call Dean, that he would be the first one to venture down the stairs, closely followed by myself. If there was a dead body or worse, he was in charge and should therefore be the one to discover what unpleasant emanation beheld us.

To say the place was a mess would be an unexaggerated understatement. Fleas the size of cats — well nearly anyway — plus a host of other wildlife that had no place being in a flat intended to be occupied by human beings.

But that was not the worst of it. The smell was absolutely horrendous and appeared to be emanating from the cupboard under the stairs. Dean stealthily eased the cupboard door open, and we were driven back by the stench. He quickly closed the door again before we both ran up the stairs retching and afraid to breathe. Outside, we gasped like two asthmatics, anxious to rid our bodies of the awful odours.

Dean had a couple of respirators in his van and so we donned those and dared to venture back into the premises. Carefully picking our way through to the cupboard, Dean opened the door armed with a torch. What beheld us was almost unbelievable. A hole had been dug in the cupboard under the stairs and had been used for some time as a toilet.

The flat was locked up and a specialist cleaning firm was employed to clean and fumigate the premises before any work could be carried out by any of the trades. It transpired that a member of staff subsequently spoke to the manager's wife and found out that they became convinced that the upstairs was haunted and would not go up there. Happy days!

*

Some people will find the above disgusting and hard to believe that it is true. Well, you can rest assured that it is true, but it is not unique. I have worked in many places where you put down your toolbox and it starts to walk across the floor — rhetorically of course. It has never ceased to amaze me at the conditions that people will willingly live in.

Admittedly the children of certain families know no better but surely any adult must realise their mistakes. Apparently not.

The worst premises that I ever had the misfortune to have to work at was a council house in Quinton, Birmingham, the area where I was actually born.

The neighbours had been petitioning for some months to have the family removed and eventually Birmingham city council evicted them – much to the joy of almost everyone in the street.

According to the neighbours, the occupants were a woman of about 24 stones, her husband, a very thin, noticeably short man and their six children, ranging from 16 years old to a toddler. Apparently, the parents spent most of their time either in the local public house or the bookies. The children were left at home almost every day to fend for themselves.

The house was that bad that if you walked up the front path, the smell would hit you, like a boxing glove in the face, by the time you were within 10 yards (this was pre-decimal) before you reached the front door. It really was that bad.

The house had to be fumigated twice and even then, the smell was horrendous. Almost everything in the house had to be replaced. This included doors, architraves, skirting boards, floorboards, light switches, and power sockets. The kitchen sink must have been blocked for some considerable time and all the kitchen waste had been dumped through the kitchen window. This comprised tea bags, vegetable waste, newspapers, and soiled nappies.

The soiled nappies were obviously a part time fixture as apparently the smallest children often walked around with nothing on and urinated and defecated wherever they happened to be at the time. The eldest girl, who had learning difficulties, was known, if she saw a neighbour outside, to pull down her kickers and excrete on the window.

At least one member of the family must have been paid regularly to *'distribute'* free weekly newspapers. The word distribute was obviously not in their dictionary though as when the loft hatch was removed, it was discovered why the upstairs ceilings were bowing downwards. The loft space was almost full to the top, of free newspapers, bundled up, just as they had been delivered.

Needless to say, it was a long time before Birmingham council were able to re-let the property and even then, there was a permanent stain, on the wall, below the kitchen window, standing tribute to the family that had moved on to who knows where?

No one seemed to know where they had gone but everyone was concerned about six children growing up, not knowing any better! Beware – They walk amongst us!

*

Once upon a time (I know it sounds like a fairy story, but I can assure you it is true) I did a fair amount of work for a Jewish, self-made millionaire. Nice bloke and fairly generous.

One day he asked me to change the fluorescent light fitting in his garage at home. Easy-peasy, thought I. I told him that I would have a look in the next few days to see what size it was and arrange to do the job as soon as possible. During the next few days, I rang his wife and arranged to go over and find out the details. It was a large garage but empty and therefore would be only a fifteen-minute job. This duly done, I ordered the necessary light fitting and arranged for a further visit to change it.

Arriving at the house I was treated to a nice cup of tea and a chat before embarking on the small job. I was handed the garage keys and after fetching the step ladder and the necessary tools, opened the garage door, only to be confronted by a car parked directly underneath the light fitting that needed attention. But not just any old car! Oh no. This was a brand spanking new, shiny Aston Martin

DB6. Right where I had to work.

On reflection, I should have walked away and arranged to do the job another day like any sensible person. I mean this was a car that was not only mega expensive but the waiting list to buy one from the factory was around two years.

After attempting to ring the owner, I was informed that he was unavailable all day. What to do? I put the step ladder adjacent to the car and found that I could indeed reach the light fitting by stretching across. Not wanting to incur a wasted journey that could not be charged for I opted to go for it – carefully.

Very steadily draping a clean dust sheet across the top of the car, I commenced the operation of removing the old light. Eight feet long and not too heavy under normal circumstances, the old light and the replacement suddenly became extremely heavy and cumbersome. It is indeed fortuitous that I used the dust sheet, as the amount of perspiration dripping off the end of my nose would surely have been enough to mark the immaculate paintwork.

After about thirty minutes of sweating, swearing and intense worrying I managed to finish the job and switched on the new light in order to admire this venerable feat of engineering. Of course, envy never even entered the equation. After all I would never even get the opportunity to drive such a beast, never mind own one.

After returning the garage keys and assuring his lady wife that everything was completed, I made a mental note to have words with the owner of the car when I next met him and ask him to ensure that a situation like that never arose again.

The opportunity to tackle the subject arose just a few days later when I was summoned to his office to replace some electrical equipment.

Upon entering the premises, I was approached by the gentleman who said, 'Thanks for doing that light in my garage the other day, it is so much better. Was everything okay?'

I answered, 'Well, it was a relatively easy enough task... but... please could you ensure next time that there is not more money's worth sitting underneath the light than I will see this year?'

'Oh yes, sorry about that but if you had asked my wife, the keys were just in the house. You could have driven it out of the garage. In fact, you could have gone a spin in it if you had so wished.'

There was a loud thud as my chin hit the floor. It is not very often that I am left speechless (as testified by those that know me) but I just stood there gawping and dribbling. My imagination was running riot as I saw myself at the wheel, roof down, hair flying back (I had some in those days), slowly waving to the passers-by.

I was suddenly brought back to reality by the sound of voices and once more stood there like an idiot in suspense, as he said, 'It is only a car after all.'

I informed him that it was probably just as well that I had not known that, as jumping from an old Transit van into a supercar would undoubtedly have been bad for both of us.

Well, we are all allowed to dream, and he did pay well for a job well done.

*

One day I had to meet up with the inspector from the local electricity provider regarding a job that needed to be done. When he turned up, he had a grin across his face broader than the Irish sea.

Upon enquiring as to the reason, he looked so happy, he related the following story.

He had just come from a premise in a seedy part of Birmingham where he had been summoned by the owner of an Asian 'Sweatshop'. Run by a gentleman of Indian or Pakistani origin, they manufactured all sorts of clothing, to be sold cheaply on Saturday markets etc.

Apparently, the factory was absolutely full of industrial sewing machines, all laid out in lines, with little room to manoeuvre in between. There was very little overhead lighting, and the heating was so inefficient as to be non-existent. The din of all the machines clattering at once was all that could be heard. A gloomy atmosphere for anyone to work in at the best of times.

The reason for the visit by the inspector became apparent as he was showed around the factory.

'I need to cut down on my electricity bill,' said the proprietor.

'Well, that could be difficult,' replied the inspector. 'The only electricity consumption seems to be the sewing machines themselves. Obviously, you cannot make clothes without them, so there is truly little to be done.'

'Well, perhaps we can run the machines on a cheaper tariff?'

'Looking at the paperwork, the only cheaper tariff would be the night tariff, whereby the electricity is consumed during the off-peak hours overnight.'

The owner of the establishment did no more than put his hands in the air and shouted at the top of his voice, 'Stop all the machines now. From now on we are working nights instead.'

It was at this point that the inspector picked his chin up off the floor and vacated the premises, totally gobsmacked at what had just gone on. I often wonder if they continued working the night shift.

*

Whilst working on the Esso site in Stoke-on-Trent, the builders came across an electric cable. When I say came across, it actually appeared as it was ripped out of the ground by the mechanical digger. Many digger drivers are only too aware of the terrific explosion caused as such cables are ripped in two or severely damaged because no one knew they were there. As the resident electricians on site, we were summoned over to seek advice as to whether it was alive or dead and whether it was important.

Three of us sauntered over to inspect the cable which was still draped precariously over the bucket of the digger. It was obvious to us experienced people that it was undoubtedly a high-tension cable. That meant high voltage, which in turn meant – run like the wind before it blew up.

We knew that it was not anything to do with the site wiring and the only viable option was to contact the local electricity board and request that they investigate it as it most likely belonged to them.

The following day a team of inspectors and other workers turned up on site armed with all the correct drawings and equipment. After around three hours of umming and arring, head shaking, telephone calling and chin scratching, it was the conclusion that nobody had a clue whatsoever what it was or where it went.

The only option left to try was 'The spike'. This involved strapping a hydraulic machine around the cable, standing well back and activating a huge steel spike that would penetrate the cable thereby causing a short circuit of the cables inside. If there was electricity actually going through the cable it would cause it to explode which in turn would cause a fuse to blow or a circuit breaker to trip. This would then identify the origin of the cable and steps could be taken to repair and identify it. If it was not alive – well it saved the cost of a spike.

The necessary equipment was not available until the following day however and so the digger was left unavailable for a second day. This did not please the contractor, but the digger driver refused to operate the machine until he was confident that he was not going to get fried to a frazzle.

The following day, the equipment in question arrived at site along with the workmen to dig around the cable and operate the machine.

They duly dug a suitable trench around the cable, strapped on the machine and stepped well back. Armed with ear defenders, goggles, hard hats, steel toe capped boots and high visibility vests, they looked pretty impressive as the atmosphere among the other workers on site reached an anticipatory crescendo. Nothing this exciting had happened on site since one of the lads had nearly severed a finger while digging a trench.

I know, we were a sad bunch, but that is life on site most of the time. That is why events, such as listed beforehand in this book are often the highlight of the week.

Anyway, the moment of truth came around as we all stood, hands over ears, far away from the cable, as a loud bang was heard as the spike was launched through the cable. Everyone held their breath waiting for an explosion of epic proportions. As we all fell on the floor, one by one, gasping for breath, it became blatantly obvious that that was the shattering anti-climax. The cable was indeed dead. Fortunately, none of us were, as we all, breathing normally again, made our ways back to our jobs.

The only good that seemed to come from this was the fact that I was the one that was asked to go and remove the cable so that the builders could get back on track. Fortunately, I have always been a 'tatter'. That is to say I always collected any scrap metal I could lay my hands on and would weigh it in once or twice a year to fund the lifestyle that I wished to become accustomed to (dreaming is allowed even if it never came to fruition). So, I had a word with the digger driver, and he resumed pulling up the cable to a point where I could saw off a good-sized piece, allowing him to continue digging out his trench and enabling me to haul off a sizeable chunk of copper cable to add to my collection.

*

A related tale involved an extension being built on a factory premises in Birmingham. I had received the drawings and submitted a price for the necessary works that had been agreed. One day shortly after pricing up the job I received a telephone call saying that my presence was required on site as soon as possible as there was a problem. I knew that the extension could not possibly have been built in such short a time and so took a trip to site as soon as I could.

The site foreman met me and explained that whilst digging out the foundations, the mechanical digger had once again come across a large cable that needed attention. Being completely unfamiliar with the premises, I had no inkling where the cable originated or terminated. After questioning various members of staff, and management, it was thought highly likely that it was a redundant cable that years before served a remote structure, but no one was absolutely certain.

The site foreman explained that it was crucial that the cable was either re-routed or completely removed the next day as it was impeding progress of the build. The following day being Saturday, no one was working on site or indeed in the factory and I would have free rein to do as needed.

Now, I did not have access to any such equipment as hydraulically driven spikes or drawings showing possible routes of cables. All I had was my trusty tools and my intuition. I also hired an industrial style detector as used by the utility companies to identify cables, pipes etc. underground. This should at least determine if the cable was alive or dead and hopefully serve to identify the said offender. If it were dead then it could be removed and if alive, I had suitable materials to re-route it sufficiently for the ground works to continue. Happy days indeed.

I attended as promised the following morning, being allowed access by a member of staff who had volunteered to attend. The weather was pretty atrocious – cold and drizzling of that exceptionally fine rain that soon gets you wet to the bone – great, just what I needed. Inside the factory was a cable that looked very similar to the offending item and appeared to head in that direction. It had been disconnected some years earlier apparently and the general consensus of opinion was that this was the cable in question. I attached the necessary piece of equipment to the end of this cable that would send a signal down it. Then all I had to do was wave the magic wand over the cable in the trench, hear the signal, cut off the cable and retire to the peace and quiet of a nice cosy fire and watch the six nations rugby.

Happy as a pig in the proverbial, I walked over and commenced waving my equipment about (I can hear your filthy minds already) waiting for the signal. An eerie stillness accompanied the sound of silence as I frantically waved it about (you are at it again!). Nothing! Absolutely not a peep. Strange, I had convinced myself that I had found the right cable, and all would soon be done. After checking the internal connection, I tried again and again but to no avail. Carrying the detector inside I checked the cable where I could actually see it. Nothing, Zero, Zilch, Nada. Just effing great, the bloody thing did not work. I had been assured by the geezer in the hire shop that it had been tested and worked as needed.

By this time I had not got time to exchange the detector as the shop would shortly be shutting and the man with the keys was anxious to lock up and take his wife a good husband – providing he could find one on the way home that is.

There was only one solution left. Cut the cable with a hacksaw – that is right a metal hacksaw. If it was dead – problem solved. If it were alive – would I be? In theory, the saw would be in contact with the metal armour that was inside the cable and if it then encountered a live cable, cause a short circuit, blow the relevant fuse and be dead before me. Yes, there would be a big bang, but I would be spared. That is unless someone had put a nail across the fuse – see chapter 16.

Faced with no alternative, as the keyholder was impatiently peering around the doorway, I tentatively stood in the trench and proceeded to saw the cable in the centre. I was very soon soaked, partly from the rain and partly from the sweat that was by now running down the crack of my bum. Nervously sawing, I reached the point where I knew that the crescendo was imminent. It was like a soldier trying to defuse an unexploded bomb, (well it was to me anyway) as I awaited the outcome. Pretty soon I reached the climax (not that sort) or should I say an anti-climax.

It was becoming obvious to me that the cable was exposed enough to be in a position where if it was going to explode, it would have done. It was indeed dead as a dodo. With renewed vigour I sawed off the cable at both sides of the trench, returning home to watch the rugby with a nice little earner, my hacksaw intact and still more copper to add to the pile.

*

By now you may have gathered that I enjoyed collecting scrap metal. In fact, I still do it now. In the garage are bags of brass and copper, although that is as far as it goes, no lead or aluminium etc. as in days gone by.

I was not the only one that liked to earn a bonus by collecting the odd piece of cable here and there. But some of the lads took it to another level.

One of the apprentices that I worked with never left a single inch of cable lying around. He spent an inordinate amount of time wandering around with a sack collecting every tiny scrap of copper cable. One time he was on a large site, working away from home, whilst gathering any odd offcuts of cable plus any short pieces of copper pipe left by the plumbers on site. Any money gained from it would be turned into a boozy night out for the lads on site courtesy of Tommy.

During the afternoon break, all the lads were in their respective huts having a well-earned rest and a cup of tea when the foreman electrician rolled up in his car and strolled in. This guy was a new addition to the firm and was keen to show everybody that he was in charge. He was destined not to last very long in his position as he had an uncanny knack of upsetting everyone he encountered.

As he entered the hut his eyes were furtively scanning the men, as well as the piles of materials. He spied an open sack leaning against the rolls of cable and went over to investigate. Peering inside, he could see that it was almost full of short offcuts of cable, obviously someone's stash of 'Tat'.

'Who does this belong to then?' he said.

'It's mine,' said Tommy.

'Wrong answer,' replied the foreman snarkily, 'it belongs to the company you work for. Please put the sack in the boot of my car and I will take it back to the yard.'

'You are joking!' scoffed Tommy.

'Do you see me looking happy?'

'That will be the day,' piped up an anonymous voice from the back.

'Who said that?' said the irate foreman as a sea of blank faces peered back.

Pointing at Tommy he snarled, 'Do as I told you now or you will be looking for a job by the end of the week.'

Tommy knew he had no choice but to obey the orders of the 'Kamp Kommandant' and stood up holding out his hand for the car keys. Pocketing the keys to the foreman's car he hefted the heavy sack up onto his shoulder and slunk out of the shed. Five minutes later he returned, gave back the keys and sat down to finish his break. At this, the foreman turned on his heel and left the shed stating that any further scrap cable should go the same way as this haul in future.

'That is a bit of a bummer,' said one of the lads. 'Now all of the scrap will have to go back to the yard in future. Bang goes our nights out freebies.'

'I don't think so,' smirked Tommy. 'I am no pancake expert, but I know a tosser when I see one.'

'How come we are still in for our little treat?' came a little chorus of voices.

'Well, he said to put the sack in the boot of his car. That is what I did. But I emptied it before I put it in, so the scrap is over in the toilet. And according to him that is where the rest has to go as well.'

Tommy never had to buy a drink that night as he related to the rest of the lads what had happened.

One of the directors visited site later that week relating matters of insubordination among the workers. By the time he left, he was in no doubt about the attitude of the new foreman and how he seemed to delight in upsetting the workforce. Apparently, this was not the only negative report received about him and his face was never seen on that site again.

*

It was always a controversial matter exactly who the scrap metal actually belonged to, but a blind eye was normally turned as it was not worth getting picky about… normally.

On one occasion, some lads were replacing a considerably long length of exceptionally large cable throughout a factory. The new cable had been installed and the old one was being removed. I am not sure who was actually to reap the benefits of the scrap copper, but the instruction was to cut it into two-foot lengths and stack it in a far corner of the yard outside. No problem – the order was followed and a pile of sections of cable was coming along very nicely.

Roughly halfway through the removal, one of the lads came up with a great idea.

'If we take a van load into the scrap yard ourselves, no one will be any the wiser except us and we could be onto a nice little earner,' said Johnny.

'I don't know,' said Jimmy. 'We have our instructions, and we could get into trouble. I cannot afford to lose this job; I have a mortgage to pay, and my wife is expecting a baby.'

'Exactly, you are going to need a little extra cash. Nobody will know and they are not going to miss one van full.'

Johnny knew a little scrap yard only a few miles from where they were, so they decided to nip down at lunch time to scope out the owner regarding a van full of cable. They duly went down to the scrap yard during their lunch break.

'Hiya mate,' shouted Johnny, above the sound of cars being crushed. 'Would you be open to some scrap copper cable coming in?'

'Yes, we deal in all sorts here mate. It is legit though, isn't it?'

'Of course, we are working up the road at... and mentioned the name of the factory.'

'Sure, when do you want to bring it in?' asked the scrap yard boss.

'How about after work tonight? About five thirty be okay?'

'That would be fine. We close at that time so if you can make it no later, I will hang on five minutes.'

'No problem, we will be here on time,' stated Johnny, feeling elated.

On their return they parked the van where it could not be seen and would be easy to slip in the odd length of cable discreetly. Whistling away, Johnny and Jimmy went back and forth armed with lengths of cable. One for you, one for me! One for you, two for me.

Temptation and greed often lead to disaster and surely enough it was not too long before the back of the van was nearly scraping the ground. Five o' clock rolled around, and it was time to get the show on the road.

Fortunately, the lads had been at the factory for so long that the security on the gate knew their van well. Waving goodnight to them, he never seemed to notice the van struggling to crawl up the road weaving from side to side as Johnny struggled to steer the overloaded vehicle.

Eventually rolling up at the gates of the scrap yard, Johnny reversed the van in and opened the rear doors. 'Here you are mate,' quipped Johnny, feeling incredibly pleased with himself.

At this juncture out popped two very dapper looking gentlemen. 'I am arresting you two on suspicion of theft,' said the one.

The other one gave them the necessary spiel about their rights before they were handcuffed and shown to the office where they awaited the police van. They were duly taken to the police station where they were questioned and placed in secure accommodation for the night. No further action could be taken before the morning, when the management of the factory could be consulted.

Unknown to Jimmy, Johnny was not a stranger to the inside of a police cell. He came from a family of travellers and had been a bit of a rogue in years gone by before a spell in prison had made him see the error of his ways and he had vowed to keep out of trouble. For many years he had become a reformed character and learnt a trade that helped him keep out of trouble. Just seizing an easy opportunity had led to his downfall. Meanwhile, poor old Jimmy sat swearing and sweating in his cell unable to believe his luck and frightened of the bollocking he was going to receive from his wife when he eventually got home.

All this was revealed the next morning as the lads were given a good talking to before being told they could leave. Apparently, the factory that they had been working at manufactured metal goods of various types. This involved several different metals and all the scrap yards for miles around were under notice for metal emanating from this source. If Johnny had not mentioned the source of the material and not forewarned the boss of the scrap yard of the delivery, everything would have been okay, and the nice little earner would have been received.

As it was the lads were dropped off at the scrap yard to retrieve their van and given instructions to return to the factory and report to the board room as soon as possible. Upon arrival at the gates, the security guards reluctantly admitted them, amidst scowls of hatred. They had been given warnings after allowing the van to come and go without searches of any kind and were lucky to keep their jobs albeit on probation.

The lads made their way up to the board room where they were admitted, to find their boss sitting with the head of the factory. They were duly informed by the factory gaffer that he had spared them a police record (No, not 'Dancing on the moon'!) by not pressing charges, but they were not allowed to enter the factory gates after they had left this time. Following that telling off they were informed that they would be transferred onto another site and were lucky to keep their jobs. Furthermore, a close eye would be kept on them in the future following a written warning.

Breathing a very large sigh of relief, the lads left the board room, returned to the van, and drove back to the company headquarters where they were given directions to separate sites. Oops! There but for the grace etc. But not all questionable decisions turned out too bad as can be seen below.

*

Sometimes things turned out well for some of us and not quite as well for others. One day a certain newsagent's company that we did a lot of work for acquired a new premise that had been trading for many years, run by an elderly couple. No, they were not elderly for many years but had been there for so long that they were a part of the furniture. He had woodworm and she had creaky joints, and both were falling apart – it sounds a bit like me now actually. The shop and the living quarters, which were above, had had no money spent on them for an awfully long time and consequently needed a considerable upgrade before they were suitable to represent a prestigious company.

As the shop was still trading, it was decided that the living accommodation would be stripped out and made suitable for when a new manager was appointed. Someone went and did a preliminary survey, and it was decided that the first job to be done was a rewire as this entailed making a mess. My brother was sent over to start the rewiring and I was to join him later that day to assist.

Upon entering the premises, he looked around and decided to start in the loft area where the cables could be run around freely. Tentatively raising the loft hatch, which had obviously not been moved for a number of years, he peered into the gloom of the loft space – or tried to anyway. Turning on his torch, he shone the light into the space – or tried to anyway. Except there was no space as he could identify. Shimmying further up the ladder, he attempted to see over the piles of boxes that were obscuring his view but to no avail. The whole of the orifice that he could see into appeared to be absolutely full of cardboard boxes. Thinking that they were surely empty, he attempted to move one or two, but it transpired that they in fact had unknown hidden contents.

He rang head office and explained the situation and received the advice to carry on with any preparation work that he could, and they would send the maintenance man around in the morning to empty the loft. Also, he was asked if he would he mind giving the guy some assistance to vacate the space. This seemed a reasonable request especially as there was a financial incentive for his assistance.

As it happened, I was held up on another job that day and was unable to offer any help on the rewire until the following morning.

The next day the three of us turned up as did a rather large skip. The maintenance guy, Danny, had had instructions to dump all the contents of the attic into the skip and leave the space clear for us. At first the boxes were removed and after a quick firtle through were deemed to be rubbish such as Christmas decorations, stationery, old paperwork for the shop etc. between the three of us, the skip was slowly filling up. Danny decided that another skip would be required and got on the phone to the skip hire company to arrange a change over. By the time we were on the second skip, the boxes had obviously been stashed away for some considerable time.

Each box was given a quick inspection before being assigned its place in the skip and before long it was noted that some of the boxes contained more than rubbish.

Cigarettes and cigars by the boxful were starting to come out as were boxes containing sweets and toys. Danny checked with head office and was informed that all the tobacco products were to be retained as the duty paid on them could be reclaimed. All other items were to be thrown out.

It soon became clear that some of the *'rubbish'* was indeed worth keeping as diecast model cars were discovered along with electric train sets and Scalextric racing sets. All brand spanking new, all still in their boxes and some sealed in cellophane.

Obviously, Danny kept the lion's share, but our kid and I managed to siphon off a fair number of Dinky and Corgi models. We all went home that night feeling rather happy with our stashes. We eventually left Danny to finish off hauling his *'stash'* and went home to sort out whatever we had managed to wheedle out.

Some months later, as I was undergoing financial difficulties, I decided to start listing my cars, Airfix kits and sets of soldiers on Ebay to ease the coffers slightly. I was really surprised to find the amazing prices that some of them were commanding. I decided that a little homework was in order and set about researching the remaining items. Some of the rarer items I took to a local auction house, to sell at their premises and others were once again consigned to Ebay. My financial situation was alleviated for the present time at least. Happy days!

A few weeks after I happened to bump into Danny. I suppose I should have looked where I was going but *'C'est la vie'* as they say in all the best French movies. Anyway, after exchanging the niceties that are usually swapped by contractors worldwide, things like, 'How are you, you knock-kneed knackered old rat bag' and 'How are you going Shithead' (other greetings are available but not usually as polite) the subject got around to the stashes of swag that came out of the loft. I explained to him that I had hit financially hard times and succumbed to selling off my share. He then told me how he still had all his in his spare bedroom (posh git).

'I still have the diecast models, in fact there are over 300,' he said. 'Fortunately, I dumped all the boxes off them in the skip just in case anyone from head office happened along,'

I looked at him askance, unable to utter a profanity for some seconds.

He in turn looked bewilderingly at me and said, 'What is wrong with your face?'

'What is wrong with my face? My face cannot believe what you just said!'

'What? I had to make it look as if it was just rubbish being discarded if anyone happened along, so I threw in all the empty boxes. I still have all the cars, so the value is still there. I was considering selling some soon to finance a holiday for me and the wife. In fact, if you could give me some clues as to how I could reap the maximum benefit from them I will buy you a pint later.'

I managed to haul myself up off the floor where I had collapsed in an unsightly heap and clarified the situation discreetly for his delicate shell-likes. 'You F*c*ing idiot, you F*c*ing decimated the F*c*ing value by at least F*c*ing half by F*c*ing throwing away the F*c*ing boxes.' Very succinctly put if I say so myself.

'What do you mean?' pleaded Danny. 'I still have all the models; I only ditched the boxes.'

I sat him down on the nearest available chair and spelt it out to him, slowly and mainly, where possible, in words of one syllable, that the boxes were in fact worth as much. If not more than the actual toys themselves. Especially when they were absolutely immaculate as those were.

'Are you sure?' he whispered.

'Absolutely. You consider that the cars etc. are all made of metal and so millions of them remain, in all sorts of condition. The boxes were only cardboard, and many were discarded after being opened, and the remainder are very often tatty to say the least. Boxes in really good condition are collectable in their own right. With the relevant model inside they are highly sought after.'

'You are pulling my plonker aren't you?' asked a face that was starting to comprehend the consequence of the owner's actions.

The thought absolutely repelled me, and I very much doubted if it would have recompensed for his losses anyway. Plus, the fact that I am definitely not that way inclined. 'Does this face look like it is telling porkies? And I definitely do not even want to go within two feet of your plonker, thank you.

I do not like to see a grown man cry, so I took my leave of the gibbering wreck that was sitting, head in hands, attempting to flood the premises with his salty emissions. I meant his tears, for those of you that cannot help themselves.

It was some months later that our paths crossed again and through a tear misted face Danny explained that he had indeed sold his share of models through the same auction house that I had used. Although he had not realised the true value that he may have done at one time, he nevertheless had himself 'A nice little earner'. Apparently, he had told the auctioneers that he had come across the collection as they were, without boxes. And he still had a few train sets and racing car sets. Those were still intact, and he was in discussion with the same company about selling them.

Like I said – *'C'est la vie'*.

*

Employing people was, I have always said, one of the worst parts of being self-employed – see chapter seventeen. I knew that as soon as my back was turned, they would be sat on their arses, drinking tea apart from *'borrowing'* my materials and equipment from site to carry out their own jobs at the weekend. I know this to be true as I was once employed by others. I am not naïve enough to believe that all my employees only lived to worship me and carry out my instructions without question or hesitation.

So long as the jobs were completed in a reasonable time span and professionally, I was content to give a little slack. I know the one lad I employed use to spend two hours in the pub every lunch time. I also know that he turned out more work in a working day than any of the others, so therefore nothing was said.

I always tried my best to look after 'the lads', taking them all out about once a month for a meal and perhaps ten pin bowling or suchlike. Unfortunately, this did not assist in keeping them loyal. At the first sniff of a *'better prospect'* most of them were willing to up sticks at a moment's notice and jump ship. I was almost constantly on the lookout for good, reliable labour.

On one occasion, I was beavering away in the office when the phone rang. I answered it and was told that it was a guy from Walsall Council. I immediately perked up thinking that a possible work opportunity was headed my way. It never mattered how much work I had in hand more was always welcome. Even when it was physically impossible to fit in any more at that time, every time I said no it came out as yes. At the back of my mind were the times when there was a dearth of jobs, and a wage was only a rant to someone who could not pronounce their aars.

Anyway, this chap on the other end starts wittering on about some certificate that I had issued for a council owned property. There appeared to be a problem with the safety side of the property even though I had supposedly signed off on it. I racked my brains diligently for any remembrance of the property or the job and approximately two nanoseconds later explained that I had no recall of any such memory. He then went on to explain that he had the certificate in front of him, duly signed by myself.

I, at the time, had to pay a substantial amount of my hard-earned money, as well as prove my aptitude, each year to the NICEIC. This stands for the National Inspection Council for Electrical Installation Contracting, the ruling body that any self-respecting electrical contractor belonged to. This still stands today. Any electrical contractor that is trading without membership of this institution should start wearing a feathered headdress as I believe that they are getting rid of the *'Cowboys'* on Friday.

After sorting through both of my brain cells again, I was still unable to remember any such place or project and asked if he could fax a copy of the certificate through to me and I would look at it (yes, this was in the days of fax machines, before scanning and e-mails, slightly after the demise of the dinosaurs). This he agreed to do, and I settled down to what I was engrossed in before the telephone rang.

After a while, the fax machine whirred and sprang into life. Surely enough it was a copy of a NICEIC certificate. It certainly made a change from letters from Nigerian chiefs explaining that I could be the recipient of millions of pounds for letting them use my bank account. If only I could have remembered the account details, then it would have made redundant the need to write this book in order to try and raise a few Sheckels.

I perused the certificate and checked the number. Each certificate number was unique and again cost a considerable amount of money. Certain that the number was not one that was issued to me, and the signature was not mine, I rang the geezer at the council and explained this to him. He, in turn, questioned why my company name appeared on it. To this I had no explanation at all and said I would carry out any further investigations that I possibly could.

I contacted the NICEIC and spoke with their fraud department. At least I was pleased that my money was being invested wisely. Life carried on as normal and the matter was forgotten by myself, until a letter arrived one day, out of the blue (actually I think it was delivered by the postman) informing me that the matter was formally investigated and with the assistance of Walsall Council, an electrician from Walsall had been identified as having carried out work for various bodies under my company name.

After sifting through my memory banks, I remembered the name. It was a fellow who had phoned me one day asking if I had any work. He had been given my name by the sister of a cousin, who was friends of a bloke down the pub (a bit like all these experts on Facebook nowadays).

After a conversation on the phone and me being overloaded with work, I decided to give him a chance – my opportunity of philanthropy – and he had sub-contracted to me for a couple of weeks before suddenly not appearing one day. Despite repeated attempts I was unable to contact him (even the carrier pigeon returned stamped 'unavailable'). Giving up on him altogether I was surprised when he contacted me a fortnight later. He explained that on his way to my house one morning he had encountered a patch of black ice (other colours are available) and the next thing he remembered was waking up in hospital where he was kept for a few days before being sent home to recuperate. It actually transpired that he had a job to do of his own, that he did before crawling back to my benevolence. I found this out some months later through a mutual acquaintance.

He obviously remembered or made a note of my unique NICEIC number and had somehow acquired a quantity of certificates from somewhere. The NICEIC declined to prosecute him at this point, although they had apparently issued him with a very severe warning of trying to repeat the exercise at any time in the future.

It was approximately twelve months later that I received another letter to say that he had indeed ignored their advice, issuing more certificates under my name and number. This time they were, rightly so, prosecuting him for fraud. They also asked if I would be prepared to act as a witness. I said that would be absolutely fine as long as I did not have to go from door to door preaching and handing out copies of the *Watchtower*. I am not sure of what became of him after this time as I was never asked to appear and can only presume he pleaded guilty. Hopefully, he learned his lesson after being tasered, hung, drawn and quartered and then given three hundred years in solitary confinement. Let no one say that I am not a humane person, but I do believe that justice should be carried out to its fullest extent.

*

Whilst working in South Africa I had a rather unfortunate experience one day. I was working at a nationalised iron and steel industry plant. The plant itself covered approximately twenty-five square miles, which is bloody big believe me. It had its own bus service and if we wanted to go to the canteen any time, we had to either catch the bus or get a lift in the company pick up. The raw materials, coal and iron ore came into the one end of the plant and iron bars, sections, billets etc. came out by lorry from the opposite side.

I worked in the billet mill which in itself was an absolutely massive building. Beneath the building was a series of tunnels where all the electrical cables and pipework were situated. It was often necessary to go down in the tunnels for either working or whiling away a few hours when there was no work pressing. In order to prevent stagnation of the air in the tunnels, gigantic fans situated at one end, constantly pushed a passage of air through and consequently it was relatively comfortable when the temperature outside was in the thirties and the humidity in the nineties. The rat population down there was multitudinous. They were everywhere, where it was mainly dry. The wetter areas were taken over by the frog population (that is to say, the hoppy creatures, not the French residents). Many hours were spent catching the frogs for a friend to use as fishing bait. Because of the rat population, cats were encouraged and fed all around the plant area.

One day, a couple of us were sat drinking tea in the mess room (and it was a mess) around mid-morning, when the foreman waltzed in with a worksheet.

'Here you are lads, a nice easy little job for you to occupy a bit of time,' he said. 'There is a funny smell emanating from somewhere, around the electrical switch-room down in the south quarter.'

'Hang on a minute, we are electricians, not drain engineers,' I volunteered.

'No, apparently the smell is in the direct vicinity of the electrical switchgear, so go and have a look will you. It may be something arcing across or burning out,' he replied.

'Okay, we will go and have a look.'

Fortunately, he had had the foresight to bring the keys to the department's pick up, so off we swanned to the canteen. Nothing like steak and chips to set you up for another hard day's skiving. The canteen was subsidised by the company and beef in South Africa was not only relatively cheap but delectable tasting, so therefore steak and chips was usually the breakfast of choice. After a hearty meal, washed down with copious amounts of tea and fags (cigarettes, that is, not homosexuals as in the United States of America) we drove down to the nearest entrance and walked to the switch-room in question.

Now when electrical equipment has a loose connection somewhere and causes overheating leading to burning, it has a pretty distinctive aroma. As we neared the area in question, it was blatantly obvious that this was not an electrical smell, per se (no, not you Percy). It was indeed an obnoxious stench originating from the bus bar chamber.

I will, at this point attempt to explain a bus bar chamber. It has nothing to do with public transport or potties that you wee in. It is a large steel box that contains heavy copper bars that distribute electricity from the incoming main cable out to the other bits. Comprehend? No, I thought not but anyway you can take my word for it, you do not want to go poking your fingers around inside it.

I am not sure about you, but I am allergic to electricity, as I have found out on many occasions, not least in chapter seventeen. But we were electricians and we had been sent to investigate, so investigate we would. Tentatively, we unscrewed the front cover and lifted it free of its restraints. Immediately we were bowled over by the horrendous pong that metaphorically smacked us around the chops.

'What the hell is that?' We uttered in unison (it was possibly in falsetto, but there you are). We placed the cover on the floor and peered inside. There, splayed across the bus bars was a ginger cat – fried to a crisp (a little like the Chinese menu in some establishments that I have patronised). It was obviously dead and had been that way for some considerable period of time.

'What are we going to do with that?' I ventured.

'That is easy,' said my colleague. He had worked there for a few years, unlike me who had only been there a short time. 'It's a job for the boys, that one.'

'I thought we were the boys,' I replied.

'Come with me. You are in South Africa now. You do not lift anything heavy, and you do not get your hands dirty.'

At that we returned to our own little enclave in the maintenance department.

This all took place in 1976 when apartheid was at its height. I will say no more on this sensitive (to some people) subject other than to voice my opinion that it was a far more prosperous country in those days. Almost everyone could find work if they so desired, not like the present time.

In the maintenance section was a mess room specially for the black workers. This is where my colleague, Johnny, took me for my first time. He knocked on the door (very polite of him) and walked in. Around a large table sat a gaggle of black workers, feasting on the brains of a sheep, the skull of which was sitting forlornly in the centre of the table. Overcoming my desire to introduce everyone present to my partly digested steak and chips, I stood there as Johnny said, 'Right, I want a volunteer to do a small job. You will do.' As he pointed at one of the guys.

Johnny turned around and left, beckoning me to follow. I duly followed him back to the pick-up truck, closely followed by the other guy who promptly jumped in the rear. Back we went to the switch-room where, surprisingly, the cat was still splayed out. The smell had not abated, and we all stood there gagging.

'That animal needs fetching off there. I would suggest you find a wooden stick from somewhere as those bars carry a lot of electricity and you do not want to touch them, believe me,' said Johnny to the Bantu.

In turn he looked at Johnny, mouth wide open and almost going white and said, 'Oh Boss, I cannot touch that.'

'It is no good "Oh Bossing" me. The job needs doing and you have been nominated. If you can do it without blowing the place up, or yourself, I will give you a cigarette.'

That was obviously the magic formula as I could not see his arse for dust as he flew through the long grass, searching like a bloodhound on a trail, for a suitable stick. Two minutes later he was back with a suitable long, dry tree branch. Deftly using the stick like a surgeon operating on a patient he prised the remains of the pussy away from the bars, balanced it on the stick and disposed of it in the long grass. Johnny and I screwed on the cover while he was away.

Beaming from ear to ear, he returned and was rewarded with a whole cigarette that he proudly smoked on the way back. He thought it was all his birthdays rolled into one to have a whole fag. The norm was to smoke your cigarette but leave an inch or so unsmoked and throw it on the floor where it would be retrieved and finished for you. Different times, but who can say whether they were better or worse?

*

Sometimes it was necessary to carry out a job out of normal hours – as in chapter six. Sometimes it was a pub or maybe a bank but more often than not it was a convenience store. Refurbishments were often needed to keep the stores up to date as needs evolved. Although some of the work could be carried out during normal trading hours, certain jobs needed to be done when there were no members of the general public around.

It was particularly amusing when, although the front door was locked and the whole store in turmoil, some low life would try and do their shopping. After trying the front door – locked – they would try rattling it to see if they could unlock it that way. All the lads would stop work and just stare at the window licker standing outside.

Next would come the knocking on the door and the plaintive cry of 'Are you open?'. This would normally occur after the local pubs had ejected their dregs out onto the street. Some were inebriated, others were of a mentality that shadowed an amoeba.

The normal reply would be to the effect of 'Of course we are open, that is why the front door is locked'.

This would then elicit another shaking of the door along with 'Could I have a bottle of milk?' or 'Can you get me some tea bags?'

The ensuing cry would normally be unprintable but would inevitably something along the lines of *'Go away in short jerky movements you brainless son of unmarried parents.'* That of course is the abridged version. Normal service would then be resumed whilst the brainless son of unmarried parents carried on asking for their shopping until such time as they got fed up and went home or collapsed in an undignified heap on the pavement. We were always very careful to tread over them on the way out after completing the works.

*

Well, I think it is time to wrap up this masterpiece. There are other things that come to mind occasionally but I must save them in case this becomes a best seller and I receive a literary award. The need for a follow up would then become necessary. Unfortunately, if it took as long as this one to write, I would be eligible to enter the *Guinness Book of Records* as the oldest person to have ever lived. I doubt that this will ever happen but, in the meantime, I will continue to support the publication by carrying on drinking their famous stout.

I hope you enjoyed reading it as much as I enjoyed writing it. Actually, I hope you enjoyed reading it more than I enjoyed writing it as at least you will have gained something from it. I on the other hand will not grow rich from the royalties, but I do have the satisfaction of completing it – at long, long last!